A Handbook for Episcopalians

A HANDBOOK
for
EPISCOPALIANS

By

WILLIAM B. WILLIAMSON
M.A., S.T.M., D.D.

Rector, The Church of the Atonement
Philadelphia, Pennsylvania

MOREHOUSE-BARLOW CO.
New York

To
three active and loyal
partners in a quest
Blanche
David
Ruth Anne

Acknowledgments

A Handbook for Episcopalians had its beginnings in a personal and family quest. As a convert to the Episcopal Church, I early felt the need for such a book. Later, parishioners' requests were answered with a series of lectures and sermons on the various subjects involved. Finally, through the co-operation of Mrs. Ruth S. Shea, parish secretary of Trinity Church, Williamsport, Pennsylvania, some sixteen of the chapters were mimeographed and used for confirmation instruction and for general information.

To acknowledge all sources of assistance would be impossible. Some benefactors, however, merit special recognition. The Right Reverend Frank William Sterrett, D.D., LL.D., sometime Bishop of Bethlehem, was at all times a true apostle, a concerned pastor, and a warm Father-in-God, who guided me in the early days of the quest.

The generous and indulgent parishioners of St. Stephen's Church, Catasauqua; Grace Church, Honesdale; Trinity Church, Williamsport; and the Church of the Atonement, Philadelphia, have all contributed understanding and encouragement along the way.

Chapters 11, 12, and 25 are revised from articles published in *The Anglican*. Chapter 25 was also published in *The Witness*.

The Glossary was prepared in collaboration with my son, David, who helped me write definitions which were not too erudite and clergy-like. The work was read and suggestions made by Mrs. Harriet Rettew and Miss Marion Maynard. Critical help was supplied by John S. Holland and Kenneth C. Slagle, Ph.D., in the areas of content, grammar, and construction. In addition to Mrs. Shea, Mrs. Maryann Moon Peck, Elizabeth Gardiner Wallace, Florence Edzell Lindsay, and Mrs. Martie Wright Lobb have provided necessary secretarial assistance at various stages of development. The author wishes to acknowledge particularly the enthusiasm and generous assistance of Patricia A. Harley, whose skillful guidance and diplomatic counsel brought rewarding improvements in content and style throughout. My family contributed heavily toward the work, helping in critical comment, reading, and proofreading in addition to their many sacrifices to the cause of producing this volume.

W.B.W.

Philadelphia
Trinity, 1961

Contents

A Handbook for Episcopalians

1

Why Choose the Episcopal Church?

WHY CHOOSE THE EPIS-
copal Church? Indeed, why choose *any* church? Several reasons
are often given as the common experience of many people.
The Church guides and strengthens the religion of individuals. Without a channel through which religion may be expressed, increased, and renewed, individual religion would
have no continuity nor depth. In the Church millions of adherents have found the most rewarding source of fellowship
and acceptance experienced in a community which worldly
sources cannot match. The Church provides a vital mission
to the world in which each member is called to serve and
share for the spread of Christ's Kingdom (Book of Common
Prayer, p. 291). The Church is a most effective stimulant in
every aspect of social religion, promoting mutual helpfulness
and common concern within its special and unique community.

True and acceptable as these reasons are, they are all incomplete. The only valid reason for choosing the Church is
that it was founded by and upon Jesus Christ, the Son of God.
The Church is not a philosophical society, nor a club, nor a
voluntary religious federation of like-minded members. The
great confession of St. Peter, "Thou art the Christ, the Son
of the living God" (St. Matthew 16:16), reflects the true con-

fession of the deity of Christ on which our Lord said He would build His Church. The foundation of the Church is established and grounded in the primitive Gospel—Jesus Christ's life, passion, death, resurrection, and ascension. The Church was not invented by a few of the more enthusiastic followers of Christ. He was the Church and into fellowship with Him He drew those who believed and would follow. A man once said to Thomas Carlyle, "I'm ready to found a new church." The answer of the great philosopher and author was, "Fine, all you have to do now is to live as no man has ever lived, die as no man has ever died, rise from the grave, convince your followers of a great mission, and live among them always. Then and only then will you be ready to found a new church."

Why choose the Episcopal Church? Three answers are outstanding. *First, the Episcopal Church is part of the Apostolic Church founded on God's mighty acts in Jesus Christ.* There is no such thing as "Episcopal religion." The Episcopal Church carries on the Apostles' rich heritage and full tradition in "doctrine and fellowship, and in breaking of bread, and in prayers." This compact listing of the minimum elements of Apostolic character and teaching was made by the author of the Acts of the Apostles (2:42). Following such Apostolic religion faithfully, the Episcopal Church qualifies to be called catholic and the Church of the Creeds. The Apostles' and Nicene Creeds, which state the full faith of the Church, are the only Episcopal doctrinal standard. The Nicene Creed has been called the "national anthem of the Christian Church," which actually it is. As the "communicants' creed" it remains the fullest expression of the Church's faith.

The Episcopal Church has made no additions to Apostolic faith, as has the Church of Rome. Nor did Anglican reform-

ers make any subtractions from the full faith and witness of
the Church, as did the reformers responsible for many Protestant denominations. Using as our guide the Holy Scriptures,
the Church's book with its rules and standards for our faith,
and depending upon the inspiration of the Holy Spirit, the
Episcopal Church continues to uphold the universal faith,
"which was once delivered unto the saints" (Jude 3).

We also continue true to the historic ministry directly descended from that of Christ's chosen Apostles. The bishops
are our historic continuity. Chosen and commissioned as were
the Apostles of the early Church, our bishops are consecrated
by the laying on of the hands of three other bishops. The
Episcopal Church continues to ordain men to the priesthood
in an historic and valid manner. All who are ordained to the
Episcopal ministry are commissioned officers in Christ's army,
commissioned by those who were commissioned by the original Apostles who were themselves commissioned by our Lord.

Episcopal worship retains the Apostolic emphasis of the
breaking of bread and the use of prayers, following the example of the early Church. The two major Sacraments which
we teach and use were ordained by Christ Himself—Holy
Baptism and the Holy Communion. We regard them as God's
ordinances, channels of God's grace through the Holy Spirit,
administered by the Church. Following the instructions of
our Lord we continue our worship in prayers, corporate and
private. His prayer is used in every one of our services as it
was used in the very ancient Church.

*Second, the Episcopal Church is continually a Church for
today: conservative and yet modern; Catholic and yet Protestant; reformed and yet liberal.* In other words, the Episcopal
Church continues unhindered its contemporary tasks: to
preach and teach the Gospel, to dispense the Word of God,
and to administer God's Sacraments to the people. This is

primitive Christianity reflecting the attitude and teaching of the Master "to serve the present age."[1] The Episcopal Church is at once a Church of creedal nature and of evangelical spirit. We are a confessional and evangelistic Church. We believe repentance and faith to be the way of new life in Christ. We believe in a redemptive community wherein each is witness to the truth of his own personal salvation and the corporate salvation of all those who believe in Christ.

The "church for today" offers challenging opportunities for service through personal and corporate works and gifts. Christ still asks for all of a man—all that he is and has. There is no modern substitute for the missionary spirit of giving all, beginning with self, to the cause of Christ. The Episcopal Church is an available channel for the eventual reunion of Christendom. Our Anglican Communion testifies to the basic unity already existing of the family of Christ. We have been called the *Via Media,* the "middle way," and rightly so, because we maintain true catholic tradition and helpful reforms.

Third, beautiful and liturgical worship is an admitted attraction of the Episcopal Church. Every service answers the challenge of the call to confession in Morning Prayer "to set forth his most worthy praise." Often people ask, "Why is the Episcopal service so outstanding?" The answer is that we have true corporate worship based on the Book of Common Prayer and arranged with but one purpose: to worship God in the "beauty of holiness." The Prayer Book contains all three elements of true worship: prayer, praise, and precept or prophecy. None of these elements is overdone or neglected. Each has its proper place. The Prayer Book maintains the worship attitudes of the early Church in "prayers" and is strictly faithful to Apostolic teaching and practice.

The biblical content of each Prayer Book service is greater

---

[1] From a hymn by Charles Wesley, "A Charge to Keep I Have."

by actual comparison than that in the services of many other churches. The Sacraments claim a central place in the faith and worship of the Episcopal Church. Holy Baptism, the initiation rite, and Holy Communion, the strengthening and refreshing rite of the Church, each have more significance than ordinary forms of public worship and prayers. The Prayer Book is written in classical English. It is dignified and reverent, carrying with it all the advantages of such a superb book. Through the Prayer Book each worshipper may follow and use in common the outward expression and substance of his worship. Anglican worship is almost the same all over the world because of this book.

The Prayer Book means so much to Episcopal individuals and families because it is comprehensive, speaking to all their needs and to all the varied areas of their lives. It is both suggestive and satisfying. In arranging a service for German prisoners of war I once used an adapted Prayer Book service, having nothing available in German. After the service one of the German prisoners said to me, "It is good to be with God again." Even though the language was not his own, he felt the universal and personal appeal of the Prayer Book.

As a convert to the Episcopal Church, I have been asked frequently why I chose the Episcopal Church. My personal reasons provide a most adequate summary.

I chose the Episcopal Church because it does not compromise the Christian faith. The faith it teaches is a faith "believed always and everywhere by all men." Essential Christian doctrine is not watered down by the Episcopal Church. The Incarnation, the Resurrection, and the Ascension—indeed, all the facts of the Gospel (the Good News)—are our heritage to believe and to proclaim. It is stimulating and reassuring in our age to say, "I believe." It is encouraging in a world torn by Communism and by threats of annihilation to believe as

St. John taught that faith will overcome the world. Much good can come to all of us if we remember that the Church is an anvil that has worn out many hammers.

I chose the Episcopal Church because it is the most adequate modern representation of the Apostolic Church. The historic Episcopate has been preserved for us through an unbroken succession of bishops from the Apostles themselves. No man founded the Episcopal Church. We have no confession to sign nor system of theology dependent upon one man's invention or teaching. We have bishops, but we are democratic withal. The Archbishop of Canterbury is the presiding officer of the Anglican Communion and not the head of the Anglican Church, nor does he claim infallibility. It is said of the archbishop (and of all his brother bishops) that he is always right except when he is wrong. This attitude toward ecclesiastical authority makes the entire Anglican tradition helpful, modern, and democratic.

I chose the Episcopal Church because it provides the most inspiring worship possible. Our worship is God-centered, not clergy- nor choir- nor even Bible-centered, even though the Bible makes up a good part of our services. At the center of Episcopal worship is God. As a United States Army chaplain I felt frustrated acting the role of a "religious master of ceremonies." Concerned about standing thus before men who needed contact with God directly, I adapted the Prayer Book service of Morning Prayer for use as a "general service." Many men immediately voiced their appreciation of this change, saying they felt deeply the value of personal contact with God. "We know now that we have worshipped God," they would say.

If you choose the Episcopal Church you will know the happy rewards of success in your search for a warm church home, a sincere fellowship within the Apostolic Church. You will benefit from a new life in Christ, and fuller life in the family of God. Remember too, however, in choosing the Episcopal Church you assume the responsibility to know and to proclaim a living faith in Jesus Christ, and you must answer the challenge to speak out for Christ's Church.

Questions for Reflection or Discussion

1. How would you explain the Episcopal Church to one who inquired about it?
2. Discuss the statement: "One faith is as good as another."
3. Answer: "A person does not need the Church to be a Christian."
4. What would you say to a person who said he didn't believe in the Church because it contained so many sinners?
5. How is the Church much more than a local organization of Christian people?
6. Answer the criticism that Episcopal worship is "too formal."
7. Answer the challenge: "Apostolic tradition is not too important; it is more important to get the work done."
8. Describe how the Episcopal Church is truly a part of the Apostolic Church.

Books for Further Reading

Bernardin, J. B., *An Introduction to the Episcopal Church.* Morehouse-Barlow. New York. 1940

Johnson, H. A. (Ed.), *This Church of Ours.* New York: Seabury Press, 1958 (pamphlet).

Pike, James A. (Ed.), *Modern Canterbury Pilgrims.* New York: Morehouse-Barlow Co., rev. ed. 1959

Simcox, Carroll E., *An Approach to the Episcopal Church.* New York: Morehouse-Barlow Co., 1961.

2

The Episcopal Chapter
in Church History

THERE IS BUT ONE PLACE
to begin a discussion of the Episcopal chapter in church history—at the very beginning. The history of the Church was begun when God founded the Church in His Son, Jesus Christ. Dr. Powel M. Dawley labels this fascinating ever-living subject the "story of God's redemptive activity among men through a fellowship that is no less than the Body of the Living Christ."[1] This basic definition also speaks to the modern misconception that the Church was organized by a few disciples after Christ's death to maintain His high ideals. The Church is Jesus Christ. He called, taught, commissioned, and ordained the Church to carry on His mission under the strength and guidance of the Holy Spirit.

The Episcopal Church shares the universal characteristics of the Church of the Apostles. With the primitive Church we acknowledge only one Head, Jesus Christ; only one Vicar of Christ, the Holy Spirit. Our baptism is described in the Prayer Book as into "the Body of which Jesus Christ is the Head" (p. 290). We also share the strong doctrine of the primitive Church. With the Apostles we declare, "I believe

[1] Powel M. Dawley, *Chapters in Church History* (Greenwich: Seabury Press, 1950), Preface.

that Jesus Christ is the Son of God" (Acts 8:37). As the early Church developed the Creeds, so we maintain them as standards of Christian faith. Critics say, "Away with creeds, they only divide us." We affirm that they are expressions of our very life—the Gospel. As they proclaim God's mighty acts in Christ they give us substance for unity.

This primitive insistence on doctrine also incorporates a growing dependence upon the Holy Scriptures. The Episcopal Church bases its faith upon the Bible. We turn to the New Testament to gain experience and inspiration from the early Apostles and disciples as they lived and wrote in testimony to Jesus Christ. By its "Common Prayer" the Episcopal Church has maintained and enriched the powerful primitive Christian worship. We know what St. Paul meant when he urged that by the Holy Communion we "proclaim the Lord's death until he comes" (I Corinthians 11:26, R.S.V.). Episcopal worship and Sacraments mean something ever more wonderful to each individual and parish.

The Episcopal Church shares the common history of the Church for many centuries. The Church has been called the one light in dark and medieval ages—flickering at times, yet effective. The first two hundred years tell a story of great persecution and equally great growth. Six generations of Christians lived under the shadow of death. Still the Church grew steadily and was full of great warmth and fervor, led by the Holy Spirit and the example of the martyrs. During those early centuries the Church was governed, and corruptions of the faith were dealt with, by general councils of bishops. The Council of Nicea in 325 furnished the great Creed which remains the doctrinal bulwark of the Christian Church. A later council established the canon of the Bible as we know it today.

In the fourth century the Church was given relief from official persecution by the action of Emperor Constantine, who with motives confusing to us made himself the champion of Christianity. Using the sign of the cross as his emblem, Constantine held the empire together and brought about its Christianization. With his influence Christianity was established as a state religion and thus the Church and the churches flourished. Great centers of religion had also developed in Antioch, Alexandria, Constantinople, and Rome. However, during this early period the beginnings of separation between the East with its patriarchal system and the West with its growing papal power were noticeable. This separation was accomplished in 1054 by mutual expulsion.

The period of church history which includes the Dark Ages witnessed two unusual phenomena: first, the growth of the power of the Pope, the Bishop of Rome; and second, the low ebb of popular education. These two factors were influenced greatly by the feudal system which when combined with the varied political, social, economic, and military movements of that day further darkened the air. Also in this period certain novelties and innovations developed within the Church: services in Latin only; the temporal supremacy of the Bishop of Rome, along with the developing concept of his spiritual infallibility; forced confession and forced celibacy; and the granting of papal indulgences which gave promise of relief from temporal punishment for sin. The most extreme doctrine of the rise of the papacy was the *Unam Sanctam* issued by Boniface VIII. He declared that "authority was given St. Peter over kingdoms and empires, and his successors might give them or take them away." The Church did produce some great and heroic churchmen in this period. Their names read like an honor roll of Christianity: Ambrose, Augustine, Anselm, Aquinas, Bernard, Francis.

The Episcopal Church is the beneficiary of the English Reformation. This reformation itself was not just a hostile revolution fought by a few hotheads, as Rome would have us believe. It was a movement growing from expressed needs by powerless church councils and prophetic individuals. A great reformation leader wrote, "I would have the lowliest read the Gospels and Epistles." The basic religious causes of the Reformation were deep-seated. The medieval Church was submerged in politics and wealth. Non-resident clergy and bishops enjoying freedom from civil law worked against local and national interests. The Church also took advantage of the ignorance of the people by selling relics, trinkets, and indulgences, which the unscrupulous misrepresented to the people. Along with spiritual unrest there came the rise of nationalism with new political interest, a renaissance of learning, and the planting of the seeds leading to the industrial revolution. Conflict with the temporal supremacy of the Pope was inevitable.

Actually the reformation on the continent was centered around Martin Luther and John Calvin. These leaders did not merely reform the Church of which they were a part, they established new churches. Luther emphasized the doctrine of justification by faith alone. He reformed Roman Catholic worship and put the Bible in the German tongue for all to read. Calvin developed a great biblical theology, emphasizing divine predestination and election. Luther's *Apology* describes the feeling of the reformers: "The teaching is not mine . . . in common with the congregation of God's people, [I] hold one common doctrine of Christ, who alone is our master." Meanwhile the Roman Catholic Church, realizing the justice of the cry for reformation, called the Council of Trent, which while it reformed peculiar and secular abuses only helped to increase the power of the Pope.

The reformation in England, however, was quite different.

Through constitutional reform over a longer period of time, the Church *in* England became the Church *of* England. As early as 597 missionaries to England had found Christianity already established. Indeed, foundations of a national Church were observed at the Council of Whitby in 665. Through the years which followed, the Church in England maintained nominal relations with the Pope. William the Conqueror and his Norman clergy and bishops brought to England a greater dependency on Rome. However, even as early as the Magna Charta the Church of England was declared free and national. A long line of "catholic" reformers, including Wyclif, Erasmus, and More, moved England ever closer to spiritual independence from Rome.

What happened in the English Church? The final action was taken by Henry VIII acting in council with the bishops of the Church in England and with the Parliament. The declaration of the Church of England simply denied the right of the Pope to exercise authority over it. "The Roman Pontiff has no more power in England than any other foreign bishop." By this action the same Church remained constant although it was reformed completely. The reforms of the Church of England recovered ancient truth, worship, and discipline and were embodied in the Book of Common Prayer, which was largely the work of Thomas Cranmer. The liturgical and other resources contained therein express the creedal nature and the reformed and evangelical spirit of the Church. The authority of the Bible in matters of faith is carefully spelled out in contemporary statements and the Church of England was unanimous in declaring that the papacy has no warrant in Scripture or early church history.

It was during the reign of Elizabeth I that the Church of Rome withdrew from the Church of England by papal bull. This separation followed the establishment of the English

Church under England's constitutional monarchy. The papal edict forbade the attendance of those who remained loyal to the Bishop of Rome at the "damnable communion" of the Church of England. The paradox lies in the thirty-six years between Henry VIII and Elizabeth I, when six Popes ruled in Rome. Either the Church of England was properly Catholic during this period or else the Popes were guilty of dereliction of duty in not having acted earlier. As it was, the Church of England remained the Catholic Church in England and the Roman Catholic Church became the separated, schismatic Church.

Within a very short time the Episcopal Church was established as an independent church in America. The Church of England came early to American shores. The explorer Cabot (1497) had with him an English chaplain. Sir Francis Drake (1579) also had a chaplain on board who read a Prayer Book service on the shore of San Francisco Bay. However, it was in Jamestown (1607) that the first permanent Anglican mission was established in America. The Church at Jamestown on June 21, 1607, witnessed the first Prayer Book celebration of the Holy Communion in the first American parish by the first Anglican pastor, the Reverend Robert Hunt. Thus began the continuous life of the Episcopal Church, daughter of the Church of England in America.

Indeed, for thirteen years the Anglican Church was the only Christian Church in English America. The Roman Catholic Church had established an earlier mission in Florida (1565), but full-scale growth awaited missions in the Carolinas and in Maryland. The opening up of the new land witnessed the coming to America of men of many nations and religious groups. The European religious wars and their aftermath caused the immigration of French, German, and English to the infant Colonies. The New England colonists, of "religious freedom" fame, founded a new state in that area where Puritan religion and practice were dominant. Many Americans are tempted to be over-sentimental about the "Pilgrims." The truth is that the Pilgrims wanted complete freedom and tolerance so they could be authoritarian and intolerant.

The work of the Church of England spread throughout the Colonies in a very short time. Episcopal success in Connecticut is a most interesting story. The President of Yale College, Dr. Cutler, a Congregationalist, became convinced from his reading of church history that Anglican Orders were unquestionably valid and superior to his own. His resignation was followed by that of five of his faculty, who with Dr. Cutler were ordained in England. This splendid group returned to Connecticut where a great and continuing work was begun. However, the work in the Colonies was hampered by the lack of a bishop for episcopal oversight and for confirmations and ordinations.

The American Revolution, however, was responsible for the establishment of the Episcopal Church even though the war all but destroyed Anglicanism in America. The Church of England people and clergy were suspected loyalists. The paradox was that while some were Tories, two thirds of the signers of the Declaration of Independence were Anglicans. Of the early statesmen in America, Washington (who was a vestryman of his church), Hamilton, Madison, Henry, Franklin, Jay, Marshall, Morris, and countless others were nurtured in the Anglican Church. Postwar feelings against anything English resulted in the impoverishment of the Church of England in America. However, the movement toward the establishment of the Episcopal Church was fast and dramatic, led by two clergymen, William Smith and William White. Samuel Seabury was elected the first American bishop by the clergy in Connecticut and was sent to England for consecration. Bishop Seabury was unable to secure consecration there because he could not sign an oath of loyalty to the English Crown. He then went to Scotland where he was consecrated in 1784 by the Episcopal bishops there. Two years later, in 1786, Bishops White and Provoost were consecrated in England where new legislation had been enacted to make it possible for the Apostolic Succession to be established in America.

In September, 1785, the first General Convention of the Episcopal Church was held in Philadelphia. This convention drafted the constitution and canons of the American Church, now to be known as the Protestant Episcopal Church in the United States of America. The Book of Common Prayer was also revised to suit American attitudes and spirit. With marked Scottish influence, especially in the liturgy, the new Prayer Book was established as the cornerstone of the life of the Church. The Preface gives a clue to the nature of the Episcopal Church: "This Church is far from intending to depart from the Church of England in any essential point of doctrine, discipline, or worship" (p. v).

Thus, the Episcopal Church had begun its own history in its new land. Later General Conventions made changes in the constitution and canons and accomplished revisions of the Prayer Book. The historically sound and unchanged basic nature of the Episcopal Church remains both catholic and evangelical. Loyal to one Head, Jesus Christ; faithful to Apostolic doctrine, discipline, and worship; continuing in reform toward the primitive and unified Body of Christ; giving allegiance to no earthly person, neither pope nor reformer; offering fellowship to all Christians; adapted to a new country with new and democratic principles, the Episcopal Church meets the needs of the present and the future with a vital challenge of modern discipleship.

Questions for Reflection or Discussion

1. Explain how the Episcopal Church is both Catholic and Protestant.
2. How would you answer the person who claims that Henry VIII founded the Episcopal Church?
3. Who *did* found the Episcopal Church and who is its head?
4. Discuss the statement: "The Episcopal Church gives no allegiance to any earthly person, neither pope nor reformer."
5. What do the words *One, Holy, Catholic,* and *Apostolic* mean when used to describe the Church?
6. Discuss the four marks of the Apostolic Church, "the Apostles' doctrine and fellowship . . . breaking of bread and . . . prayers," as they apply to the Episcopal Church.
7. Even though related to the Church of England, how did the Protestant Episcopal Church become a completely independent American Church?
8. Explain to your neighbor the story of the consecration of the first American bishops.

Books for Further Reading

Clarke, C. P. S., *Short History of the Christian Church.* New York: Longmans, Green & Co., rev. ed. 1948.

Dawley, Powel M., *Chapters in Church History.* New York: Seabury Press, 1950.

Dawley, Powell M., *The Episcopal Church and Its Work.* New York: Seabury Press, 1955.

Manross, William W., *A History of the American Episcopal Church.* New York: Morehouse-Barlow Co., rev. ed. 1959.

Moorman, J. R. H., *A History of the Church in England.* New York: Morehouse-Barlow Co., 1954.

Wilson, Frank E., *The Divine Commission.* New York: Morehouse-Barlow Co., rev. ed. 1940.

3

The Episcopal Church's Creedal Nature

THE EPISCOPAL CHURCH IS most accurately described as the Church of the Creeds. As there is no such thing as Episcopal religion, neither is there Episcopal doctrine. In contrast to Lutheran and other confessional theology, Episcopal theology is the Church's doctrine given in the Creeds. It is described as "the true Christian faith which has been held in the Church always, everywhere, and by all." This universal faith is affirmed in the Episcopal Church at every service.

The modern cry "I believe in religion, but not in a creed" must be answered at the outset. The Church's answer is that the Christian cannot be non-creedal. Indeed, the Church of which Christians are part was founded upon a creed, that great statement of faith uttered by St. Peter, "Thou art the Christ, the Son of the living God" (St. Matthew 16:16). This credo was shortened to the first-century statement "Jesus is Lord." Each generation henceforth has been asked the same question, "What think ye of Christ?" Christians do not invent their answer nor the faith expressed. They bear witness to the faith made known to them by Christ in the Church, a living faith which they must also make known.

The Christian Church is not a debating society, it is the Body of Christ called forth to proclaim the Gospel to each generation. Christianity has been given great meaning and a

glorious mission because of the Creeds. They contain fundamental Christian faith and imperative backed by the Person
and power of our Lord Himself. The Creeds existed long before the canon of the New Testament was established and
thus support the New Testament completely. They continue
the work of Christ as the Church continues the work of Christ.
In the Gospel the command given by our Lord to His
Church was "Go . . . and teach all nations" (St. Matthew
28:19). The Episcopal Church continues in this teaching
mission, using the Creeds as the basic text.

Something must be said about the Creeds specifically and
historically, since they are essential to right faith. The
Apostles' Creed was an expansion of the earliest Christian
credo and grew out of the missionary life and evangel of the
early Church. A common legend about the Apostles' Creed is
that each Apostle contributed a phrase. Whether this is true
or not, we are certain that it is a very early creed. It has
long been called the Baptismal Creed because originally it
was the confession of the faith of a catechumen. It was the
pledge of allegiance of a newly baptized soldier of Jesus Christ.
Indeed, the confession of faith in baptism often signed the
death warrant of the early churchman. St. Augustine, discussing the vital nature of the Apostles' Creed to the early
Church, said, "This Creed of few words is made known to the
faithful so that by believing it they may be subdued to God . . .
they may live rightly . . . may purify their hearts, and may . . .
understand what they believe."

The Nicene Creed has always been considered by the
Church as the bulwark of Christian doctrine. The General
Council meeting in Nicea in A.D. 325 answered the major
heresies of the day and gave, with the enlargement of the
Council of Constantinople in A.D. 381, a final statement of
orthodox Christian faith. The bishops declared, "We all be-

lieve in this, into this we are baptized, into this we do baptize."
The Nicene Creed has long been called the Creed of the
communicant. Used in preparation for confirmation and in
Holy Communion, this creed indicates the full maturity of a
Christian. The Nicene Creed contains a complete statement
on the deity of Christ and places Christ where He belongs—
at the very center of our faith.

The Church's Creeds, Apostles' and Nicene, teach us to
believe:

1. *"In God the Father Almighty, Maker of heaven and
earth."* God is the Creator. He has made us and He sustains.
God is transcendent, almighty, all-powerful, and everliving.
God is our Father. He is eternal love manifested over and over
again. God is immanent—as close to us as our breathing itself.
God is revealed to men through the Persons of the blessed
Trinity. He is one yet, indescribably, three Persons. We cannot demonstrate how this is pragmatically possible, but we
do believe in an absolute God who could make such a revelation a reality.

2. *"And in Jesus Christ his only Son our Lord . . . of one
substance with the Father . . . incarnate by the Holy Ghost of
the Virgin Mary, and . . . made man."* Here is a clear definition of the nature of our Lord. The Incarnation is indeed the
basic Christian doctrine. St. John describes this mighty action:
"For God so loved the world, that he gave his only begotten
Son, that whosoever believeth in him should not perish, but
have everlasting life" (St. John 3:16). The Creeds teach us
that God became man that we might become reconciled as
His sons. The Nicene Creed insists that Jesus Christ was truly
man and truly the divine Son of God. The mysteries of the
Incarnation are clear when we acknowledge Christ to be

eternally divine. Even the Virgin Birth seems most plausible
when we believe "all things were made by him." Finally,
Jesus most perfectly reveals the Father. The testimony of our
Lord was, "I and my Father are one," and again, "He that
hath seen me hath seen the Father" (St. John 10:30, 14:9).

3. *"Who for us men and for our salvation came down from
heaven . . . suffered . . . was crucified, dead, and buried: He
descended into hell; The third day he rose again. . . ."* The
Atonement is the chief work of Christ. The salvation of
mankind was secured by Christ's death on the Cross. The
Cross, exemplifying as it did the full force of human sin as
met by the full force of God's love, reveals God's action to
save us by His suffering in Christ. The Resurrection is the
substantiating doctrine of the Atonement and the climax of
the Christian Gospel. It is the cornerstone of the Church. St.
Paul states it vividly: "The glorious fact is that Christ *did* rise
from the dead."[1] This is the testimony of numerous witnesses
and is recorded by St. Paul in I Corinthians 15. We have
received eternal salvation, freedom from sin and death, as
benefits of the Resurrection. And because of Christ's resurrection we too shall live eternally.

The statement "He descended into hell" often disturbs and
confuses Christians; indeed, the Methodists have dropped it
altogether. Some of the difficulty arises from our natural
reluctance to believe that Jesus entered into any place of
eternal punishment after His death on the Cross. The Book
of Common Prayer comments on this delicate question with a
helpful and adequate explanation: "Any Churches may, instead of the words, *He descended into hell,* use the words, *He*

[1] I Corinthians 15:20 as translated by J. B. Phillips in *The New
Testament in Modern English* (New York: The Macmillan Company,
1958).

went into the place of departed spirits, which are considered as words of the same meaning in the Creed" (p. 15). While this rubric may not satisfy every theological inquiry regarding hell, it does explain what the word means as used in the Creed.

4. *"He ascended . . . and sitteth on the right hand . . . he shall come to judge."* The Ascension is another of the mighty acts of God. It is the fulfillment of Christ's divine life. As ascended Lord, St. Paul tells us, Christ shall reign and all things shall be subdued unto Him. His glorious reign will be the final eternal victory of God. The judgment of God is an important fact in faith. "He shall come to be our judge." This judgment is contemporary and eternal. It is well said that "we are being judged and we shall be judged."

5. *"The Holy Ghost."* The Holy Ghost is the third Person of the Trinity, described in the New Testament as our advocate-counselor and as "power from on high." The New Testament contains the record of the work of the Holy Spirit and especially of the outpouring of the Spirit of God on the infant Church. The Holy Spirit teaches the faithful the truth of Christ, makes the Church effective in her witness, and brings God's grace in the Sacraments. He is the guide and strengthener of the Christian's very life.

6. *"The . . . one . . . holy . . . Catholic and Apostolic Church."* The Church is One because it is one Body under one Head. It is One also because it continues in Christ's work —our one calling to teach the Gospel. The Church is Holy because the Holy Spirit dwells in the Church and sanctifies its members. The Church is Catholic and universal because it holds the faith for all time and for all people. The Church is

Apostolic because it continues in the Apostles' teachings and fellowship. All of these statements are taken from the Second Office of Instruction, in answer to the question "How is the Church described in the . . . Creeds?" (Book of Common Prayer, p. 291).

7. *"The Communion of Saints."* This glorious company includes all Christians living and dead. All those who are in everlasting fellowship with Jesus Christ are members of the Church Militant, the Church Expectant, or the Church Triumphant. It is within this eternal fellowship that we pray for our beloved dead that they shall continue to grow in God's love and service. The truth of Christianity is that believers are one in Christ, not only today but forever.

8. *"One Baptism for the remission of sins."* The forgiveness of each Christian is accomplished by Jesus Christ. Holy Baptism with its attendant rebirth and regeneration brings us into unity with Christ and His Church. The Holy Communion supports this regeneration and gives the Christian continual strength. Confession and absolution, which are a part of every service in the Episcopal Church, express man's continued search for Christ's forgiveness and the "amendment of life."

9. *"The Resurrection of the body (dead) . . . and the Life everlasting (of the world to come)."* The Church teaches us that we will be resurrected as Christ was resurrected. The message of Easter and the Burial Office assure us that we shall receive eternal life in Christ. The Church does not teach the immortality of the soul. The Church teaches the resurrection of the body. St. Paul tells us the resurrected body will be a spiritual body and the gift of God, for "flesh and blood cannot inherit the kingdom of God" (I Corinthians

15:50). Through Christ we will inherit God's gift of victory over sin and the grave. We may join with St. Paul in the triumphant thanksgiving song, "Thanks be to God, which giveth us the victory through our Lord Jesus Christ" (I Corinthians 15:57).

The Episcopal Church is the Church of an acknowledged creedal nature. Every service offers us opportunity to respond to God's mighty acts by stating forcefully our faith in Christ. This faith expressed in the Creeds is the only surety equal to the crises of life. Such faith and such victorious living rest upon our faith in Jesus Christ. Christian faith is victorious. Thomas Carlyle once asked Bishop Wilberforce, "Bishop, do you have a creed?" The bishop answered, "Yes, and the older I get the firmer that creed becomes under my feet. One thing bothers me, however, the slow progress the creed makes in the world." Thomas Carlyle answered, "But if you have a creed you can afford to wait. You have a platform upon which you can stand and no world convulsion can shake it down." Truly, when we can say "I believe," we have hold on something worth living and dying for. The faith of the Church expressed in the Creeds puts us in tune with the power of God. With consummate confidence in Jesus Christ we can expect ultimate victory.

QUESTIONS FOR REFLECTION OR DISCUSSION

1. How would you answer, "Doctrine isn't important today, I say it doesn't matter what you believe"?
2. Why is the Church so necessary to the support of our faith?
3. Discuss the statement: "The Episcopal Church is truly the Church of the Creeds."
4. How would you answer a child who asked what God was like?

5. How can you prove the doctrine of the Holy Trinity?
6. How was Jesus Christ both truly man and truly the divine Son of God?
7. Explain the following words: Incarnation, Atonement, Resurrection, Ascension.
8. How is faith in Jesus Christ the guarantee of everlasting life?

BOOKS FOR FURTHER READING

Doctrine, Church of England. London: Society for Promoting Christian Knowledge, 1938.

Moss, C. B., *Answer Me This.* New York: Longmans, Green & Co., 1959.

Pike, James A., and Pittenger, W. Norman, *The Faith of the Church.* New York: Seabury Press, 1951.

Simcox, Carroll E., *Living the Creed.* New York: Morehouse-Barlow Co., 1950.

Wilson, Frank E., *Faith and Practice.* New York: Morehouse-Barlow Co., rev. ed. 1941.

4

The Episcopal Church's Evangelical Spirit

THE EPISCOPAL CHURCH IS both catholic and reformed in fact; it is truly evangelical in spirit. The message of the Episcopal Church is fundamentally the same as that of the Apostolic Body of Christ—the eternal Gospel, the primitive Christian Evangel (Good News). We hold a timeless heritage. As the late Archbishop William Temple aptly observed, "The Gospel is true always and everywhere, or it is not a Gospel, or true at all." Indeed, the eternal Gospel, the proclamation (kerygma) of the whole counsel of God revealed in Christ, is the Episcopal Church's evangelical message. Four dogmas make up this dramatic proclamation:

1. *The Incarnation,* which describes and documents God's self-revelation in Jesus. St. John vividly summarizes the dogma, "The Word was made flesh, and dwelt among us" (1:14).

2. *The Atonement,* the redemption of man, in which mighty act God secured for man salvation from sin. Unable to bring about his own salvation, man has been reconciled to God through Jesus Christ.

3. *The Resurrection,* in which God raised Christ from the dead. Indeed, He will raise those who believe in Him from the dead also. St. John assures us that in Christ "we have

passed out of death into life" (I John 3:14, R.S.V.). In this dogma God answers man's most despairing cry, "If a man die, will he live?"

4. *The Church,* our fellowship in the Holy Spirit. Through the Holy Spirit, God continues to give new life and blessing to those within the society of Christ. Indeed, the Church is integral to the Gospel. Believers live in Christ and with each other in a supernatural fellowship of God's creation and maintenance.

Witness to the effect of the Gospel in human life and confession of Jesus as Lord is the necessary mission of the Church in the world. The obvious power and growth of the early Church was accomplished by a vital and relevant witness by every disciple. Their message was simply this: "Christ changed my life, He can change yours. Come into the fellowship of those whose lives have been changed by Christ." This proclamation and witness is still our task. The power of Christ to change, and of the Spirit-filled Church to mature, nurture, and sustain after this change, is an ever contemporary challenge. Only such a church can give an answer to the seriously ill woman who, when given the good news that she would not die, wrote to her pastor, "Domine, I have a chance at life. What shall I do with it?"

The Episcopal Church's evangelical emphases are the same as those of classic primitive and reformed Christianity. The Anglican-Episcopal dissent was primarily from Roman Catholic errors, additions, and superstitions, but later also from Protestant deletions and negations.

The first primitive and reformed emphasis is on the authority of the Holy Scriptures. The evangelical spirit of the Episcopal Church places prime importance on the Bible to Christian faith. The Lambeth Conference has declared:

"Neither Bible nor Church is understood apart from the other."[1] The Episcopal ordination charge is classic Christianity. "Are you persuaded that the Holy Scriptures contain all doctrine required as necessary for eternal salvation through faith in Jesus Christ? . . . Will you . . . banish and drive away . . . all erroneous and strange doctrines contrary to God's Word?" (Book of Common Prayer, p. 542). The Episcopal Church teaches the Bible as the vehicle of God's message of reconciliation. Of course Jesus Christ is God's ultimate Word and the unity of the Scriptures. As a matter of fact, the Church teaches that all Scripture is to be interpreted in the light of Christ from Old Testament promise to New Testament fulfillment. The ministry of God's Word runs through all of the Prayer Book. The "comfortable words" of the Holy Communion assure each worshipper of his salvation in Christ. Such "words" must come to mean as much to us as they did to our Bible-loving forefathers.

The ministry of preaching is not neglected in the Episcopal Church; indeed, Episcopal sermons are usually mostly expository and evangelical. St. Paul's watchword is our standard: "We preach not ourselves, but Christ Jesus the Lord" (II Corinthians 4:5). As ambassadors for Christ we use God's Word to apply revealed truth and the Gospel to our daily lives. A Methodist friend of mine once called me after returning home from church to report, "Unitarian sermon today." This could rarely be a criticism of an Episcopal sermon.

Believing in Christ and inspired by the Holy Spirit, the Church becomes part of the Gospel, the embodiment of the Body-Word. The Church must live by the Bible. We grow by the Word of God. It has been said: "Whenever a single individual, layman or theologian, has been able to draw fresh

[1] *The Lambeth Conference Report 1958* (Greenwich: Seabury Press, 1958), 2.3.

and full out of the Bible and to present to others what he has obtained, the inward life of Christendom has been raised to a higher level."

The second primitive and reformed emphasis is on the doctrine of justification of a Christian by faith. The reformers used the phrase *the priesthood of all believers,* but by this they did not mean that each would be his own priest. The strong emphasis on justification by faith was set in contrast to Roman ecclesiastical imperialism. The common primitive Christian experience is most personal. First we recognize our need for God's aid, acknowledging that we are "off course," ruled by sin and self-will, and that unaided we cannot change ourselves. Second, we must accept the redemption available from God in Christ as a free gift of God's grace and reconciliation to full and harmonious relationship with Him. Third, by our confession of faith and our personal acceptance of Jesus Christ as Saviour and Lord we achieve our personal justification. There is no substitute in Christendom for a confession like that of St. Peter who, when asked by our Lord, "Whom say ye that I am?" answered emphatically, "Thou art the Christ, the Son of the living God" (St. Matthew 16:15-16). Of course, there are several varieties of New Testament Christian experience following the confrontation of a person with the Person of Christ. St. Paul is an example of a sudden complete change—conversion—which still happens. Lydia was a seller of purple and one that "worshipped God." Attracted to Christ through St. Paul, she became a disciple. St. Timothy developed his strong Christian faith under the steady and prayerful influence of a Christian home. Regardless of variety, each found personal living faith through Jesus Christ.

The third primitive and reformed emphasis is on the sanctity of the common life. The evangelical concern for the consecration of all life is in sharp contrast to the Roman concept of sacerdotalism (belonging to the priestly office alone). Indeed, our Lord Himself was interested in all life and spoke often to the world's oft-quoted fallacy that "religion is all right in its place." The faith of the primitive Christian impregnated all of life. It was said of the Christians of that day, "what the soul is to the body, Christians are to the world." The Lambeth Conference has advised, "The mission of the whole Church is to be the Body of Christ, and, through all its members, to show forth Christ to the world. . . . For Christians nothing can ever be merely secular."[2] Christian witness at home, at work, and at play, indeed at every point of human contact, is absolutely essential. We are called to be lay apostles, to witness to men where they are; to keep Christ before men in the shop, on the golf course, in politics. Martin Niemoeller was told by Hitler to "mind God's business and let me run the nation." Niemoeller answered, "God has entrusted the Church with the responsibility for the nation and no one can take it away."

The fourth primitive and reformed emphasis is upon the need for ever contemporary evangelism. The Church has always been most vital under an evangelical program. The word *evangelism* confuses many. One helpful and catholic definition has been rephrased from a Church of England report: "The presentation of the Gospel of Jesus Christ in the power of the Holy Spirit, that men shall accept Christ as their Saviour and serve Him as their King in the fellowship of Christ's Church."[3] For many, evangelism is the process of "making Christians more Christian." It is a program with dynamic to strengthen and arouse those already in the Church to greater heights of

[2] *Ibid.*, 2.113-114.
[3] *Towards the Conversion of England* (Toronto: J. M. Dent & Sons, Ltd., 1946), p. 1.

life and witness. For some, the unconverted or the pagan, evangelism is the elemental confrontation of persons with the Person of Christ in such a way that they may be converted and restored. Evangelism must be used always for the building up of the Church, not merely for "saving" people. The New Testament knows nothing of solitary Christians. The Apostolic message was "repent . . . be baptized" (into the Church). For individual primitive Christians conversion was always followed by membership in the Body of Christ, the Church.

The Episcopal Church is a worshipping, working, and witnessing evangelical community. There is wholesome and moving evangelical spirit in Episcopal worship. The Prayer Book service is rich in Scripture, reverence, faith, and corporate witness. Simple and yet catholic, it confronts and proclaims. A young soldier speaking of Episcopalians once said, "To these people religion is a beautiful and moving thing." He was right. The quiet reverent attention of Episcopal worship is most gripping.

There is strong and available evangelical necessity of work in the Episcopal Church. As the fellowship of sharing, helping believers, the Church is at work in the world. John Wesley has aptly described this evangelical attitude of mission: "Christianity is essentially a social religion; to turn it into a solitary religion is indeed to destroy it." The Church answers an individual's hunger for personal acceptance and then offers him opportunity for service, recognizing his gift as one contribution among many to the one Body.

There is also the challenging and irresistible evangelical necessity of witness incumbent on the Episcopal Church. As of old the Holy Spirit will move the modern Church to vital witness if we ask for His help. Jesus Christ who was crucified for us is alive today and demands our answer to the question,

"What will you do with/for Christ?" The Episcopal Church with true evangelical spirit is for many a central fact of faith offering a new life, avenues of prayer, Bible study, and opportunity of witness to the good news to all. William Temple describes the Church's mission thus: "Christ wrote no book; he left the world as his witnesses a 'body' of men and women upon whom the spirit came . . . the living society—the Church —was to be the primary witness."[4]

QUESTIONS FOR REFLECTION OR DISCUSSION

1. What do the following words mean: evangelism, Gospel, primitive, reformed, justification?
2. Is there a continuing personal implication in the "go" of Christ's commission?
3. How will the study of the Bible enrich the Church's evangelical spirit?
4. Are education, worship, and evangelism separate functions in the life and work of a parish?
5. Can a Christian witness for Christ and still be tolerant toward those of another faith?
6. How may a parishioner help in making his parish a more evangelical part of Christ's mission?
7. Whose responsibility is evangelism?
8. How can Communism be labeled an "evangelical and missionary movement"? Is it a rival to Christianity?

[4] *Ibid.*, p. 121.

BOOKS FOR FURTHER READING

Kean, Charles D., *Christian Faith and Pastoral Care.* New York: Seabury Press, 1953.

Phillips, J. B., *Making Men Whole.* New York: The Macmillan Company, 1953.

Shoemaker, Samuel M., *By the Power of God.* New York: Harper & Row, 1954.

Towards the Conversion of England. Toronto: J. M. Dent & Sons, Ltd., 1946 (out of print, but may be found in libraries).

5

The Purpose of an Episcopal Parish

Wʜᴀᴛ ɪꜱ ᴛʜᴇ ᴘᴜʀᴘᴏꜱᴇ of an Episcopal parish? What should any Christian parish be doing to fulfill its task in the world? Concerning these questions generations of Christians have debated. The modern Church in all its busyness has been compared to Wahlstrom's gadget. The story of Wahlstrom's gadget is most interesting. It was originally a World War II bombsight which Wahlstrom often took apart and put back together. However, he began adding clock and other parts to see what would develop. As time went on he added three thousand different moving parts: wheels, whistles, motors, etc. Wahlstrom's gadget is said to run with tremendous motion and noise, but it doesn't do anything constructive. It just runs "wheels within wheels." Is this a picture of a modern parish? Can it be said of parishes you have known that they do nothing about their basic task and mission but they do make things go? As a matter of fact, isn't this an oft-given definition of the rector's job—to make things go? How can we come to realize that running parish activities is not necessarily identical with the Church's mission?

A new theology about the work and mission of the Church has developed since the turn of the twentieth century. The Church is considered a necessary value in the community, especially when advertising real estate values. The Church is also considered a fine place for children and youth, and the Church School is named as important to the life of the community, except to many of its parents. The Church is called a pleasant activity center with a task of keeping families busy, friendly, and happy in their off moments. The Church is considered so important that everyone agrees to support all-out efforts to earn money to keep it going. These efforts take the form of drives, bazaars, dinners, and all sorts of sales. Several periodicals in the past year or two have carried notices of parish churches which served thousands of meals each year for all sorts of reasons. However, are not these efforts far from the true purpose of a parish?

Our parish organizations are hard at work on false tasks, mainly because we choose the wrong definition of the word *task*. Such busyness is described as "nice activities of nice people doing nice things for a nice (vague and indefinite) cause." The parish thus involved is no different from any other secular organization and the parishioners are no different from their pagan neighbors. Such a parish will make no spiritual demands on individuals or families, but will advertise that "this church does things!"

What should a Christian parish be doing? For an answer we might turn to St. Paul, that great first-century bishop, who speaks with ever increasing vigor to the modern Church as he did to his first-century parishes. We find in his Epistles a definite Pauline pattern for the true purpose of a parish.

A Christian parish will radiate new life in Christ. For St. Paul, Christians were in Christ as new, changed persons. This was accomplished for us in the Cross of Christ. "By grace you have been saved through faith" (Ephesians 2:8, R.S.V.). New life in Christ is accepted in Christian baptism, which is our entry into Christ and His fellowship in the Church. This acceptance must follow a profession of vital faith in a living Christ. It is further acknowledged by new and happy life within the redeemed community. We move from a personal decisive encounter with Christ to a social experience of faith within "that holy fellowship." Both give a Christian the matchless free gift of God's unearned grace. With such faith in daily life and work we radiate our new life in Christ.

A Christian parish will testify to its new faith in God through Christ. St. Paul triumphantly testified, "I live by faith in the Son of God, who loved me and gave himself for me" (Galatians 2:20, R.S.V.). This new faith is born of a new relationship with God. Christians no longer fear but are God's adopted sons in the bosom of His intimate family. This new faith is based on a new fellowship of reconciliation with God. By the operation of the grace of God in Jesus Christ, Christians are liberated from sin and thus restored to a full and eternal life. This new faith in God is also a guarantee of man's new and enduring peace with God. St. Paul has aptly written, "For he is our peace" (Ephesians 2:14), and so He is! The hymn writer M. A. S. Barber sings, "Peace I ask, but peace must be, Lord, in being one with thee!"

A Christian parish will seek to appropriate the power of the Holy Spirit for guaranteeing the effectiveness of the new life. St. Paul taught that the whole Christian life, including the Church, is Spirit-controlled. Indeed, the Holy Spirit is the dynamic in the new life of a Christian, for it is Christ Himself who comes to us through the Holy Spirit. It is the Holy Spirit who pours the love of God into our hearts and prompts us to cry "Abba, Father." It is the Holy Spirit who inspires our feeble human attempts to pray. It is the Holy

Spirit who guarantees our accomplishment of Christian graces
and the reception of spiritual gifts including the gift of eternal
life in Christ. It is the Holy Spirit who is the dynamic presence
and guide of the Church called by first-century Apostles "the
Spirit-filled community." It is the Holy Spirit who inspires the
Church to world mission, the proclamation of Christ to the
uttermost parts of the world. It is the Holy Spirit who em-
powers the Church to be the sacramental vehicle of God's
grace. In Holy Baptism we are "sealed with the promised
Holy Spirit" (Ephesians 1:13, R.S.V.). In the Holy Communion we receive the spiritual food and drink of the new
life (I Corinthians 10:3-4). The modern Christian parish will
pray and wait for the power of the Holy Spirit to accomplish
the witness of its new life in Christ.

*A Christian parish will make vital and inviting the com-
munity of the new life.* St. Paul has told us, "You are no
longer strangers and sojourners, but . . . fellow citizens with
the saints and members of the household of God" (Ephesians
2:19, R.S.V.). What does this mean for us? Indeed, Christians
are no longer strangers to God or to each other. Changed by
personal experience with Christ, baptized and confirmed believers and followers of Christ are strengthened for life and
witness by the Holy Spirit indwelling the Church and the
Sacraments. Christians are named fellow citizens with the
saints. There is much joking in our modern day about sainthood, but all New Testament Christians were considered to
be saints. For primitive Christians, grace for sainthood was
another gift of God through Christ similar to God's gift of
salvation. Christians were expected to live up to the spiritual
obligations of their citizenship with the saints. The glorious
privilege of this citizenship is that Christians are members
of the household of God. Why should it be difficult to believe

that in Christ Christians are sons and heirs, intimate members of God's chosen family, the Church? It remains our responsibility to make this community vital and inviting to those who have yet to experience the wonderful benefits of new life in Christ.

St. Paul's counsel is most helpful, yet we still must answer our original question: what is the purpose of a parish?

The purpose of an Episcopal parish is to bring God's household and family into life to make it accessible to all. Our parishes must live as Christian cells within a pagan community. The early parishes to which St. Paul wrote in Corinth and elsewhere were missionary outposts. Our parishes must again learn to lift up Christ so that God may draw all men unto Himself.

The purpose of an Episcopal parish is to touch the world with brotherly concern and love. Our parishes must be a vital and inviting family, with Christian love the most obvious sign of our new, rich fellowship. Converts will be made, people will grow in Christ, ministers and missionaries will be sent forth, all in the context of Christian love. This is why parishes do as they do. This is why choirs rehearse and sing, Altar Guild ladies clean, sew, and press. This is why the sexton sweeps, the secretary runs the mimeograph, the rector preaches, and every communicant offers something of himself or his substance. We do all this to share the blessings of Christ's love and concern with every person in the world.

The purpose of an Episcopal parish is to show forth to the world the Gospel, the Good News. Our parishes must proclaim Christ that He may not only be heard but seen today as He was in and through the first-century parish. For this task every member of our modern parishes must gain new life in Christ. Christians must know more about Jesus and develop, as St. Paul advised, "this mind . . . which was also in Christ Jesus" (Philippians 2:5). We must also have, and witness to, new faith in God "in full accord and of one mind" (Philippians 2:2, R.S.V.). We must find new and appropriate power in the Holy Spirit and live as transformed Christians under the guidance of the third Person of the Trinity. Finally, Christians will enrich new fellowship mutually within the Church. We will "put on therefore, as the elect of God, holy and beloved . . . charity" (Colossians 3:12-14). John R. Mott, late outstanding world Christian, once said, "It is our duty to see that Christ is made known. The Church has no other function."

QUESTIONS FOR REFLECTION OR DISCUSSION

1. What is the essential business of the Church?
2. Is the Church fundamentally different from any other organization?
3. What false tasks do parishes around you assume?
4. Who is really to blame when a parish encounters spiritual complacency?
5. How can a parish deepen its faith and strengthen its spiritual health?
6. Do you agree that Christian witness calls for duty twenty-four hours a day?
7. How important is it to have things going in a parish for all age groups?
8. How can modern Christian parishes become "cells in a pagan community"?

Books for Further Reading

Michonneau, Abbé G., *Revolution in a City Parish*. Westminster, Md.: The Newman Press, 1950.

Miller, D. G., *The People of God*. London: Student Christian Movement Press, 1959.

Moss, C. B., *Answer Me This*. New York: Longmans, Green & Co., 1959.

Southcott, Ernest W., *The Parish Comes Alive*. New York: Morehouse-Barlow Co., 1956.

Wylie, Samuel J., *Precede the Dawn*. New York: Morehouse-Barlow Co., 1963.

6

My Duty as a
Member of the Church

THE LIFE, WORK, AND WIT-
ness of the Church is the responsibility of every disciple. The
Church was founded upon the outstanding quality of discipleship represented by St. Peter's confession in answer to the
question of our Lord regarding His identity. The Apostle's
confession of faith, "Thou art the Christ, the Son of the living
God," was rewarded with the promise of the Master, "Upon
this rock I will build my church" (St. Matthew 16:18). The
great creedal statement of Christendom has ever been, "I
believe in Jesus Christ, the Son of God, my Saviour and my
Lord." Indeed, this has been the unique and catholic confession of the Church and remains its crucial Christian witness to
this day. St. Peter, preaching at Pentecost, was asked by those
who heard his sermon what they should do to be Christians.
His answer was simple and direct. "Repent, and be baptized"
(Acts 2:38). This meant then, as it means now, to come to
Christ in repentance and to join His Church through Holy
Baptism. Modern disciples must truly evidence primitive
faith and enthusiastically answer our Lord's question, "Will
ye also go away?" "To whom shall we go? thou hast the words
of eternal life" (St. John 6:67-68). Like St. Peter of old,
generations of disciples testify that only failure is experienced
on every hand when they choose alternatives to Christ and

His Church. Christ alone has the answer to life and eternal life.

The Church provides a fellowship for believing, practicing disciples. Indeed, the function of the Church is Christian discipleship. The first task of the Church is to win and baptize those who are non-Christian so that they may become followers of the Christ. Winning the world for Christ seems like an impossible job and the odds seem overwhelming, until we remember that our Lord taught His disciples that Christians were to be the leaven within society. He also likened our meagre resources to a mustard seed which would bring forth a great tree of faith. Overwhelming odds, indeed, but victory is in sight through Jesus Christ. The creator of the famous cartoon "Skippy" once illustrated such faith by picturing Skippy planting an acorn. Asked "Why?" by his friend, he gave a classic answer. "I wanted a tree to hang a swing on." We must learn such faith for this day.

The second task of the Church is to help Christians become more Christian. This task oftentimes seems most staggering until we remember that the fellowship, which is the Church, is a strengthening body—a redemptive community. The Church is often said to be the easiest group in the community to enter: the requirements for membership are minimal and either no "dues" or low "dues" prevail. What a totally wrong concept of church membership! Jesus Christ expects *all* a person has to offer. It has been said, "Christianity doesn't require much of a man—just all of him."

All baptized and confirmed members of the Church are confronted with the statement in the Prayer Book Office of Instruction, page 291, which discusses our "bounden duty." "My bounden duty is to follow Christ, to worship God every Sunday in his Church; and to work and pray and give for the spread of his kingdom." This is not an easy outline of duties.

It is an exacting, self-disciplining mission which was presented
to the disciples by Christ and is passed on to us through the
Church.

What, then, is my duty as a member of the Church? *First, it
is my duty to order my personal life to follow Christ's example.* What is the definition of a Christian, anyway? A
Christian is a follower of Christ. This spells out our primary
duty: to be a follower of Christ. How can you tell a Christian
as he walks down the street? It is very difficult, to be sure.
Is it possible to tell a butcher from a surgeon? In street clothes
they look alike. However, when the crisis comes and an
operation is needed, we certainly would want to know which
was the surgeon and which was the butcher. The same is true
of a Christian. When the crisis comes the Christian will reveal
his true allegiance. To accomplish our primary duty to follow
Christ the Church has some concrete suggestions to make to
us.

1. *The Church requires that we attend church every Sunday for corporate worship.* There is no other place just
   like the church. In God's holy presence and in company
   with our peers, we find strength for living and inspiration for following our Lord. The great processional
   hymn "Onward, Christian soldiers" (No. 557, The
   Hymnal 1940), with its stanza beginning "Like a mighty
   army moves the Church of God," is most thrilling and
   inspiring. It speaks of our obligation as members of the
   fellowship to attend God's Church and thus march in
   His army as soldiers of the Cross. This is not an optional
   duty—it is a requirement of the Body of Christ.

2. *The Church expects us to receive the Holy Communion
   regularly.* The Church of England recommends that
   faithful communicants receive not less than once a

month. Regardless of the time element, we know that the Holy Communion is the only corporate act given to us by our Lord and that we meet Him at His holy table. Therefore we must honor Him by our faithful and *regular* reception of the Holy Sacrament.

3. *The Church expects us to be regular in private prayer.* For a Christian, prayer is personal communion with God. While this is a little used resource in our day, it still remains our duty. In fulfilling this duty we follow the example of our Lord, who taught us a qualitative prayer and not one of quantity. When we seek to begin the practice of private prayer, we would do well to begin with the Lord's Prayer. *Forward Day by Day* and other devotional materials will provide help and structure.

4. *The Church expects us to read the Holy Bible carefully and often.* The Bible is well established as the textbook of the Church. If we use it intelligently it can be of great help to our faith and to our daily living. A mature devotional program will include Bible reading.

Second, it is my duty to provide a Christian home environment for my family. The home is basically the classroom of the faith. Therefore the Church counsels us on family religion so that we may better fulfill our duty and responsibility.

1. *We must arrange for regular, helpful family worship.* This can begin in such a simple fashion as regular grace at meals. Or we can turn to the Prayer Book (pp. 587-600) and use the services and helps there for family prayer. Or we might use devotional pamphlets such as *Forward Day by Day* or any other good devotional reading material. Of course we will find that the Bible also is a rich resource for family worship.

2. *We must teach the faith by precept and example.* The

Christian faith must be taught and caught by children and youth from parents and other adults in their environment. When children are brought up to love and serve the Lord in His Church, they are prepared for life. They come to understand what they believe and they practice their belief. We can expect little from them unless we take the leadership in this direction.

3. *We must plan for a full, happy home life.* The family is indeed happy when all join together in worship, work, and recreation. It is our duty to see that each member may share, each may love, and each may profit from the influence of religion in the home.

Third, it is my duty to play a full part in the life and work of the parish. Some work in the Church is the duty of every member. Each member has some important role to fulfill in the life and work of the parish. Furthermore, our failure to fulfill our given role is sinful. St. Paul taught that the stewardship of a disciple's time and talents be offered "With good will doing service, as to the Lord, and not to men" (Ephesians 6:7). This participating stewardship is taught by the Bible and the Prayer Book as our duty. All disciples were commissioned by Christ with the task of teaching and extending the Gospel. To teach the faith is the privilege of every Christian. How can we pass on the faith if we do not share it by teaching it to others? But how can we bring the warmth of the Gospel of Christ to others unless it has saturated our lives to overflowing?

We also play a full part in the life and work of the parish by giving money for the work and mission of the parish and for the Church's world-wide mission. Our duty to give is long established in both the Bible and the Prayer Book. The Bible teaches a tithe. The Episcopal parish asks for a subscription or pledge, some proportion of our income set aside for the work of the Church. The stewardship of our income is an extension of our faith. Each gift that we make to the Church is "ourselves" going forth to serve. It is like putting our faith to work, or, as someone has called it, "negotiable discipleship."

Fourth, it is my duty to witness to my Christian faith today in my public life. Every Christian has a responsibility to give personal missionary witness to his faith in Christ. Why should we hesitate to own the cause of Christ? It is important that we speak well of the Church and never run it down. We can also invite friends to come to church with us and make certain that they feel welcome and at home. Every Christian has a duty to witness to his Christian faith by giving unselfish, personal service to his fellow men. There is no substitute for this. The American tradition is that we pay others to serve for us, but this is no substitute for personal service. We have reared a generation of weak Christians mainly because we have lost the urge to be neighborly and do something for others in the name of our Lord. Perhaps we should start a movement in the Church to "do it yourself" in the field of service to our fellow men.

A Spirit-filled, witnessing, working Church is essential in our modern day. People are choosing and pledging their allegiance to one cause or another. They might welcome warm, friendly help from us. We must remember that we are God's public relations personnel and that we are summoned to be witnesses to the cause of Jesus Christ. To fulfill our duty as members of the Church we must be faithful, worshipping, working, witnessing disciples. We might do well to ask ourselves the question, "What would my Church be if every member were just like me?" When we begin to fulfill our duty as members of the Church, the answer to this question will be given most satisfactorily in our lives.

QUESTIONS FOR REFLECTION OR DISCUSSION

1. What is the best thing you can do as a Christian? Why?
2. Why is it the duty of every Christian to worship God every Sunday in His Church?
3. Discuss the value of the establishment of regular personal prayer and Bible study.
4. Why is a definite schedule and program essential for helpful family worship?
5. Comment on the statement: "The Christian faith is often caught as well as taught."
6. Why must every Christian assume some task in the life and work of the parish?
7. Explain the Christian concept of stewardship—our duty to give systematically and proportionately to the Church.
8. Why is it the responsibility of every Christian to give personal witness to his faith in Christ?

BOOKS FOR FURTHER READING

Bayne, Stephen F., *Christian Living*. New York: Seabury Press, 1957.

Southcott, Ernest W., *The Parish Comes Alive* (Chapters II and IV). New York: Morehouse-Barlow Co., 1956.

7

My Opportunity for Proportionate Discipleship

JESUS CHRIST GAVE A NEW and unique meaning to the concept of discipleship. What is discipleship? A disciple is a follower—literally a pupil-servant attached to a teacher-master. The modern implication of the word *discipleship* is personal adherence to a cause. Discipleship was the forerunner of the guild system of teaching crafts, by which much early professional training of physicians and lawyers, as well as philosophers and clergy, was accomplished. The close relation of the words *disciple* and *discipline* is obvious. Both words suggest self-control and self-rule, and all other qualities necessary for mastery of self and subject.

What is the unique nature of Christian discipleship? A Christian disciple is a follower of Christ, in addition to everything noted above and much more. Christ's disciples literally and actually "left everything and followed him" (St. Luke 5:11, R.S.V.). Because of their self-sacrifice, however, Christ's disciples became beneficiaries of rich fellowship with a matchless and sinless Person. They came to know the limitless power of divine self-revelation, ageless teaching, and Christ's miraculous resurrection. Further, Christ's disciples were commissioned directly by Him to share and carry on His mission to all the world. These men and their successors were to be sent to the uttermost parts of the world to preach the Gospel, to baptize, and to build His Church.

Modern discipleship is at best a proportionate discipleship. Very few could qualify if called to "leave everything"; very few can go to the uttermost parts of the world to be missionaries. However, we can offer our Lord a fair proportion of ourselves, our service, and our substance (money). Indeed, it can be said without fear of contradiction that such self-giving is the only path to true Christian discipleship. Proportionate discipleship is based on such personal self-giving. We may not leave all to follow Christ but we can be and do as much as possible in His cause.

Modern disciples are committed followers of Christ. We believe on His name. We believe that He is the Son of God. We believe that He is the Way, the Truth, and the Life. Surrendered to Him, we live in Him and thus we become heirs of a great faith which is not just another religion, but God's answer to man's need.

All Christians—not just the clergy—are called and commissioned as witnesses to Christ. The story of Pentecost told in Acts indicates that the entire company of disciples was commissioned—not just the Apostles. "They were all filled with the Holy Ghost . . . and the multitude of them that believed were of one heart" (Acts 4:31-32). Consecrated lay apostles won the day for the primitive Church. Consecrated lay apostles will do the same for the Church today. However, with the hymn writer we must sing and mean, "Take my life, and let it be consecrated, Lord, to thee" (No. 408, The Hymnal 1940).

Modern disciples are stewards of time and talent. What is a steward? A steward is literally a house warden, an administrator, a manager. Stewardship is the Christian use (administration or management) of time and talents as gifts from God. Time is a gift from God; we either use it or lose it. Indeed, once it is past time is gone forever. An impressive sundial legend from the pen of an unknown author reads:

> The shadow by my finger cast
> Divides the future from the past.
> Before it stands the unborn hour
> In darkness and beyond thy power.
> Behind its unreturning line
> The vanished hour, no longer thine.
> One hour alone is in thy hands,—
> The NOW on which the shadow stands.

Modern disciples learn to give the fair proportion of their time to Christ in daily devotions, Bible reading, service, and Sunday worship. They have learned that their life is incomplete without this surrender of a proportionate share of their time to their Lord.

Talent also is a gift from God. St. Paul's counsel to the early Christians was, "Neglect not the gift that is in thee" (I Timothy 4:14). So many church people counter with "But I have no special talent." These people are wrong. Christ's parable of the talents teaches that everyone has a talent. Obviously the size or quality of the talent is unimportant. It is the faithfulness with which the talent is used that matters most. Our Lord taught that each one is held accountable for his use of each talent. Modern disciples learn to live and serve in everything as to Him. We must offer Him what we know we can be and do in His cause. For some this means singing, for others sewing, for others teaching, for others simply expressing their Christianity in all the acts of everyday life.

Modern proportionate discipleship implies a personal missionary interest. Every member of the Body of Christ has a personal responsibility to spread the Gospel through his words, his actions, his gifts of self and substance, and his prayers. Each Christian is qualified for this task by the indwelling Spirit of God and is given obvious opportunities to perform it. If a Christian ignores his missionary responsibilities, or postpones his response to them, or leaves them to others who are, he thinks, better qualified, then he cannot properly be called a Christian.

The Lambeth Conference of 1958 stated:

> The mission of the Church cannot mean less than *the whole Church bringing the whole Gospel to the whole world.* To think of missionary activity . . . as a kind of "optional extra" to be undertaken by those who are enthusiastic for that kind of thing, is to make complete nonsense of the Gospel.[1]

Modern disciples are no less responsible for the missionary task of the Church than were the original Apostles. The modern Church fulfills its task only as it carries on the primitive Christian mission under the imperative of Christ's command to "go." There is no such thing as "foreign" missions. Christian mission starts at home and then widens out to include the whole world. We must remember that the United States was once a mission field of the Church of England and of other Christian communions. But, "What are we to do?" The answer to this question is quite elementary: be a missionary to your neighbor. Every Christian is responsible to minister to the sick and the needy, the ignorant and the pagan. Further, while you may not be able to go elsewhere in the world, you can give so that others may take your place in

[1] *The Lambeth Conference Report 1958* (Greenwich: Seabury Press, 1958), 2.66.

the Christian mission. Every Christian must take a fair share in the fighting work of the Church. The Church must ask enough of her disciples and we must learn to give enough to the work of the Church.

Modern disciples are proportionate disciples. Each gives a significant proportion of himself to God in recognition of God's gifts and his need as a Christian to give. He begins with self-giving and continues through gifts of money. But many say, "Money is my own business." The Church answers, "Yes, except when it concerns God, the Giver." Christian stewardship is a Christian's gift of self and substance—which is negotiable self—to God through Christ's Church. Such giving fulfills the call of the Church to proportionate discipleship.

The Episcopal Church teaches that each and every responsible disciple shares in Christ's mission. As responsible disciples we must put God first in every avenue of life. Therefore we must put the Church first in our financial considerations. Obviously it follows that responsible disciples must put aside a significant (sacrificial) proportion of their income systematically for God's use. The decision as to the amount must be between each person and God. Since a Christian is a steward of God's gifts, whatever we give Him must be a fair proportion and not a "tip." The modern tithe is a good suggestion for a reasonable standard: 5 per cent of a man's income given to the Church and 5 per cent divided among charities. Whatever the mechanics, responsible Christians do not give to a working budget but rather to God and a working Church. When we place our gifts upon the altar, we sing "All things come of thee, O Lord, and of thine own have we given thee." Our proportionate discipleship can make this thanksgiving true for our lives.

Our cheerful and systematic giving of self and substance is the opportunity the Church offers modern disciples to fulfill Christ's call and commission as His disciples. We begin with personal self-giving, our consecration as St. Paul has described it, "With good will doing service, as to the Lord, and not to men" (Ephesians 6:7); we continue through the giving of our substance. Placed on the altar of our parish church, our gifts are used in the mission of Christ in the world through His Church. The route of proportionate discipleship is as follows: you, the parish, the diocese, and God's kingdom—the world. It is through such proportionate discipleship responsibly offered to God that Christ's mission to the world goes on. The story is told of a young woman who wanted to be a missionary but was prevented by the death of her father and serious illness of her mother. Since it was impossible for her to fulfill her call to missionary vocation, she took a job as secretary. Yet she is a missionary! She visits in her parish; nurses Indian children in Arizona; teaches in a kindergarten in Japan; works in a diocesan office—all this because her proportionate gift is offered on the altar of her parish church. Used by her Church, her gift of self and substance is true negotiable discipleship.

> To give and give, and give again,
> What God hath given thee;
> To spend thyself nor count the cost;
> To serve right gloriously
> The God who gave all worlds that are,
> And all that are to be.[2]

---

[2] G. A. Studdert-Kennedy, *The Best of Studdert-Kennedy* (London: Hodder and Stoughton Ltd., 1947). Used by permission.

Questions for Reflection or Discussion

1. How does Christian discipleship differ from other forms of discipleship?
2. Why does the title of Christian steward apply so appropriately to practicing disciples of Christ?
3. Have we the right to say to God, "What I do with my life, property, and possessions is my own business"?
4. What are some of the personal implications of the offertory sentence, "All things come of thee, O Lord, and of thine own have we given thee"?
5. Does the Christian have a "need" to offer his time, talents, and treasure to God?
6. Is a proportionate pattern of self-giving, service, and systematic offering of substance to God a reasonable response to Christ's call?
7. Discuss the statement "to whom much has been given, of him much will be required," as it applies to you.
8. Comment on the extension of self and service through a Christian's giving money to his Church.

Books for Further Reading

Azariah, V. Samuel, *Christian Giving.* New York: Association Press, 1955.

Bayne, Stephen F., *Christian Living.* New York: Seabury Press, 1957.

Creative Choices in Life (Adult Study Course). New York: Seabury Press.

Urwin, E. C., *Religion and the Common Man.* London: Student Christian Movement Press, 1951.

8

The Vocation of the Episcopal Laity

CHRISTIANITY BEGAN AS a mission among laymen. It is interesting to note that Christ called as His Apostles "common folk," laymen. The New Testament describes the contemporary Jewish churchmen—priests, elders, scribes—as worldly-wise and deaf to His call. It remained for the common folk to hear Him gladly and to follow Him. The word *laity* comes from the Greek word *laos*, meaning "the people." The Church in adopting *laos* restricted its meaning to "the people of God." The laity actually includes all "the people of God," both clergy and non-clergy alike. As we have discussed before, Christ's command and call were given to *all* His disciples. While the Apostles were to be the commissioned officers of Christ's Church, every disciple was called to "follow me" and "go and tell." This tremendous first-century imperative was based on the power of Christ's personal contact with His disciples. Still every Christian is baptized with the sign of the cross "in token that hereafter he shall not be ashamed to confess the faith of Christ"—which is our primary duty. But the baptismal challenge calls us "manfully to fight under Christ's banner . . . and to continue Christ's faithful soldier and servant unto our life's end" (Book of Common Prayer, p. 280). All Christians are thus under oath and obligation to the never-ending cause of Christ.

The example of St. Andrew is a helpful lesson on the power of the lay apostolate. The New Testament story records that Andrew found Christ and then went to his brother Simon and "brought him to Jesus" (St. John 1:42). The name Andrew means "manly." The Venerable Bede has suggested that Andrew meant to him "Introducer to Christ." Every Christian should be an "Introducer to Christ." Of course it was easier in many respects for Andrew than it is for us today. We have reason to believe that St. Peter was ready for the call. Further, personal religion was not considered an embarrassing subject before our "enlightened time." Our modern sophistication and lack of depth in our conviction cause us to avoid the idea of being an "Introducer to Christ." A majority objection would be: "Tell someone that I had found Christ? You're mad!"

There is a Christian vocation for the Episcopal laity. Of course, some laymen serve in a more specialized office as lay readers to assist the clergy in reading the daily Offices, as their title describes. The average Christian layman, however, while not a priest, is called to know his faith, the Bible, and the Church on which it is based. Christianity is often undefended because the average Christian does not know the right answers. We believe in God, in a Christian way of life. We love the character of Jesus Christ. We like the Church, we feel it is important to our life. Yet we know no vital, consuming, dynamic faith! A large corporation expects its employees to eat, sleep, talk, and live the corporation line and product. The Christian layman is called to be the corporation man for the Kingdom of Christ, to eat, sleep, talk, and live the faith of Christ crucified.

The vocation of the Episcopal laity calls for personal and group study. The Church needs laymen prepared to state intelligently the facts of their faith, of the Bible, and of church history. Christian laymen must approach their faith and the Bible with the mind (reason) as well as with the heart (feelings). The importance of what we believe, and how strongly, will be tested by the way we meet the difficulties of our time. True and lasting Christian strength and witness develop from sound belief. The salesman who believes in his product will sell his product. If you believe the Christian faith, you will radiate and sell your faith.

A Christian layman is not a platform evangelist but he is called to be a lay apostle to witness for Christ. The word *apostle* itself means a witness of Christ's resurrection. Each Christian yearns and prays with St. Paul "that I may know him, and the power of his resurrection" (Philippians 3:10). The lay apostolate of the Christian Church is often unfulfilled because the average Christian considers himself without "gifts" for evangelism. We beg off like Moses, saying as he did, "I am not eloquent . . . I am of a slow tongue" (Exodus 4:10). Or like Isaiah, who thought himself unworthy, we say, "I am a man of unclean lips" (Isaiah 6:5). Christ can give us what we need to fulfill the vocation (or avocation) to which He calls us as laity of the Church. We believe that He can give us power to pray, study, work, and witness according to His leading. Ding Li Mei, a Chinese convert, was reputed to have brought more Chinese to Christ than any native worker. When asked his method he answered, "I pray and then Christ talks through me."

The vocation of the Episcopal laity calls for an enthusiastic witness to new life in Christ by word and work. Such witness won pagans to the early Church. The lives of first-century Christians were supremely eloquent of their faith in Christ.

The Prayer Book calls for the same eloquence of life on the part of every communicant. The Christian lives but one life, a new life in Christ. He is a new creature called by God to show forth His praise not only with his lips but in his life. Such witness is still within the power of lay apostles. "Marketplace Christianity" is that dynamic lay witness which takes Jesus Christ where men are to witness for Him and His work.

The story of an Army officer and his Christian friend is significant here. They shared many long sessions on the subject of religion. Patiently the Christian explained the faith that was in him with no passion except for his firm conviction of what Jesus meant to him. Years had passed since this opportunity to witness was offered. Finally news from the officer brought an announcement of his baptism along with that of his two young children. When asked why, he replied, "You believed, that was enough for me!" Why should a layman hesitate to talk about his faith? There is so much talk on every other subject all about us. The vocation of the laity calls for enthusiastic witness to Christ.

A Christian layman is not a pastor but he is called to extend the fellowship of prayer and the ministry of reconciliation. All disciples are urged to use the resource of prayer, especially in intercession for others. If we cannot speak to our friends and neighbors about God, we can at least speak to God about them. The story of the Christian salesman who entered into a train conversation with a stranger is most interesting. It was discovered that the stranger possessed no faith. The Christian testified to his faith intelligently but got nowhere. They exchanged cards upon leaving and the Christian offered to pray for his new-found friend who allowed "it might do some good." A year or so passed and the salesman received a letter from his traveling companion telling him that he had become a Christian and joined a church. This meeting and its lay witness had an indirect influence upon John R. Mott, a great Christian layman, who later dedicated himself to a full-time vocation for Christ.

The vocation of the Episcopal laity calls for all disciples to be lay missionaries in their daily contacts. The late Archbishop William Temple said that 99 per cent of the Church's work is done by the laity. Trained laity can teach and lead Bible study, baptism, and confirmation classes, and adult and parents' groups. Trained laity can visit newcomers, shut-ins, the aged, and others. Trained laity can assist in the assimilation of new people and marginal folk into the Church's program. All laity can invite their friends and neighbors to church—and, going one step further, how much better it would be to bring them! The testimony of the members of a large Philadelphia parish confirmation class was that the majority in the class had been confirmed mainly because a layman or a lay couple had invited or brought them to church. All laity can arrange to have the clergyman come to the home to meet friends and neighbors, especially unchurched or pagan persons.

The vocation of the Episcopal layman is to live and share in the fighting work of the Church and thus perform a real and vital ministry. There is no essential difference between clergy and other Christians. Of all disciples St. Peter wrote, "Ye are a chosen generation, a royal priesthood, an holy nation, a peculiar people; that ye should show forth the praises of him who hath called you out of darkness into his marvellous light" (I Peter 2:9). It is an old hack joke but appropriate that "clergy are paid to be good and laymen are good for nothing." Perhaps there is more to this jest than meets the eye.

The story from *Servant in Thy House*[1] of the dean of a cathedral whose relative was a lowly sewer cleaner is a helpful illustration. The dean, of course, looked down on his relative until the day he was needed because of a plumbing failure. The vocation of the Episcopal laity is to seize upon at least one of the manifold opportunities for usefulness in the Church. Laymen can find their personal opportunity in the areas of worship, prayer, service, stewardship, and work, knowing that whatever is accomplished will be done within the redemptive grace of God, to His glory, and for the building of the family of God by the people of God.

QUESTIONS FOR REFLECTION OR DISCUSSION

1. Explain why it is correct to call Christianity a religion of laymen.
2. How can a Christian's daily life be an eloquent witness for Christ?
3. What are some of the everyday situations in which a Christian has opportunity to bear witness for Christ?
4. In what way does a layman who is weak in faith and witness also weaken the Church?
5. What would you say and/or do if the rector asked you to be responsible for recruiting a confirmation prospect?
6. Is it possible for a Christian to have no concern for winning others to Christ?
7. How could your parish develop and use a lay apostolate?
8. Was Archbishop Temple right when he said that 99 per cent of the Church's work in society is done by the laity?

[1] A play written by Charles R. Kennedy (New York: Harper & Brothers, 1908).

Books for Further Reading

DeWolfe, James P., *Answers to Laymen's Questions*. New York: Morehouse-Barlow Co., 1959.

Moss, C. B., *Answer Me This*. New York: Longmans, Green & Co., 1959.

Murray, John, *The Daily Life of the Christian*. Naperville, Ill.: Alec R. Allenson, Inc., 1956.

Shoemaker, Samuel M., *Revive Thy Church Beginning with Me*. New York: Harper & Row, 1948.

Trueblood, Elton, *The Common Ventures of Life*. New York: Harper & Row, 1949.

9

The Vocation of the Episcopal Priesthood

THE SACRED MINISTRY OF the Christian Church was instituted the day Christ "called unto him his *disciples:* and of them he chose *twelve,* whom also he named *apostles"* (St. Luke 6:13). All of these men He later commissioned with the words "Go ye into all the world, and preach the gospel to every creature" (St. Mark 16:15). The challenge of the Apostolic commission "go ye" is a call to action which speaks to all disciples in every age. Indeed, modern men continue to answer the urgent call of the Church with "Whom shall we send? And who will go for us?"

Jesus Christ is the perfect pattern of the Christian ministry. Our Lord brings God to man through His own personality and saving Person. Jesus is the great High Priest, forever our Mediator before God for men. He was "taken from among men . . . ordained for men in things pertaining to God, that he may offer both gifts and sacrifices for sins" (Hebrews 5:1). The Incarnate Son of God lived among us, proclaiming the Gospel, living the Gospel, personifying the Gospel. He fulfills the world's greatest need—bringing God to men, bringing men to God. We have agreed before that Jesus Christ is the Church and into the Church He calls His disciples and Apostles. All Christ's commissioned officers serve only as His ministers and priests to be the instrument of His work and mission in the world. The call of our Lord, "follow me," changed the disciples' lives and vocations. Even the persecutor Saul was converted by Jesus to become St. Paul, the "Special Messenger" (Apostle) of the Resurrection.

It is in this emphasis on men and their calling that Christianity differs so vastly from other religions. Confucius left his classics to his followers. Buddha left a system of instructions for Buddhist faithful. Mohammed left the Koran as a guide for Moslem adherents. Jesus Christ left only His disciples—no book, no system, no classics—only men. He trained His disciples in His Way by His personal teaching and witness. He exemplified the fellowship of men with God into which He calls all disciples to share as ministers. The early Church grew, led by the army of Christ with the Apostles as the commissioned officers and all other disciples the enlisted men. This ministry persists to our modern day. All disciples are ministers, especially parents and other laity in the Church. But of the many disciples twelve were chosen who were given greater responsibility and supervision.

The ministry of the Episcopal Church is substantially the same as the Apostolic ministry. However, several questions come to mind.

First, was the ministry of the Apostolic Church planned by Christ? St. John quotes our Lord as saying to His disciples, "Ye have not chosen me, but I have chosen you, and ordained you, that ye should go" (St. John 15:16). St. John later gives the account of the first ordination: "He breathed on them, and saith unto them, Receive ye the Holy Ghost" (St. John 20:22). Jesus may not have left a blueprint for the organization of the ministry of His Church, but He did ordain the Apostles and commission them with all the disciples. No doubt He did also suggest over-all principles regarding the Church's ministry which the Spirit-filled Church fulfilled.

The New Testament account does show that three orders of the ministry were present in the early Church. There were general ministers or Apostles (bishops); local ministers or presbyters (priests); and assistant ministers (deacons). How did it all come about? The Apostles were the first order. They soon felt the need of local pastors to serve in the growing local churches and so they ordained presbyters and deacons to help them.

The New Testament reveals four successive stages in the development of the ministry. First, Acts 6:2-6 records that the first martyr, St. Stephen, was a deacon. The second stage was accomplished according to Acts 13:2 when St. Paul and St. Barnabas were added to the Apostolic fellowship. The third stage is recorded in II Timothy 1:6 when St. Timothy was ordained and set aside by St. Paul. The fourth stage reveals the creation of a bishopric in Titus 1:5 where St. Paul directs Titus to ordain.

The divine origin of the ministry of the Church is echoed in the Prayer Book Collect for the Ordering of Deacons, "Almighty God, who by thy divine providence hast appointed divers Orders of Ministers in thy Church . . ." (p. 531). As we have seen above, in the lifetime of the Apostles there were deacons, priests, and bishops, separated for religious action and commissioned by Christ through His Apostles. The age-old significance of the Christian ministry is illustrated by the Reverend Dr. W. Norman Pittenger in his book *Stewards of the Mysteries of Christ*,[1] where he tells of a young parson who when putting on his stole claimed it made him two thousand years old—*and it did!* Men called and ordained to the ministry down through the centuries have been called by God;

[1] Louisville: Cloister Press, 1945.

they have been ordained by the laying on of hands and the reception of the Holy Ghost. Their duties as outlined by the Church are to speak and act for Christ—to teach and baptize in His name. Truly ours is a missionary ministry in a missionary Church.

Second, what is the teaching of the Episcopal Church regarding the ministry? The Book of Common Prayer contains the Ordinal of the Church, which is "The Form and Manner of Making, Ordaining, and Consecrating Bishops, Priests, and Deacons." The following questions and answers are taken from the Second Office of Instruction (Book of Common Prayer, p. 294). "What is the office of a Bishop?" A bishop is a chief pastor whose duties are to ordain and confirm. He is a sacramental person, not merely an administrator. As a bishop he confirms and ordains his people within the Church in the name of Christ. Only bishops may confirm, ordain, and consecrate other bishops. This latter guarantee is a safeguard to the historic Episcopate, a continuous line of bishops coming down to us from the original Apostles.

"What is the office of a Priest?" A priest is to minister, preach, baptize, celebrate the Holy Communion, and pronounce absolution and blessing in God's name. His duties are pastoral and sacramental, for priests are ordained "servants of Christ and stewards of the mysteries of God" (I Corinthians 4:1, R.S.V.). The priest is a steward of the Sacraments. Christ is the true minister of the Sacraments acting through His stewards to impart His grace. In pronouncing absolution and blessing the priest does not speak for himself—speaking in the Master's name he bestows the grace and gifts of Christ *Himself.* The priest is a steward of the Word. He represents God toward the people of God and the people before God, united through Christ.

The minister is a channel of witness to the Gospel message of his Lord. Years ago I heard the story of a young minister who was to preach his first sermon in his first parish. He had worked long and hard on what he considered to be an adequate sermon. However, just prior to the service his mother challenged him by saying, "Jamie, say a good word for Jesus Christ today." This startled him and brought him up short. He scrapped his prepared sermon and preached one of the most eloquent sermons of his entire ministry. Here is the challenge of the ministry: that as stewards and messengers, priests should give testimony to our Saviour and King.

"What is the office of a Deacon?" A deacon is to assist the priest under the oversight of the bishop. The diaconate is a training period during which the deacon may perform restricted functions of the ministry under the guidance of the bishop. It is unfortunate indeed that this order has fallen into great disuse in the modern Church.

Third, what then is the right way of commissioning ministers? There is the Roman way in which papal authority is reflected down through a chain of command to diocesan bishops. There is the Congregational way of commissioning by other local ministers upon the call of a congregation. There is the free-church way in which ministers are commissioned by the action of local congregations. There is the Presbyterian way in which ordination and commission are conferred by action of the Presbytery. There is the Episcopal way in which ministers are commissioned by bishops with congregational support and recommendation. While acknowledging that the claims and counterclaims of others are not without merit, we claim only that the Anglican-Episcopal way is the oldest and closest to the Apostolic way.

There are great values inherent in the ministry of the

Episcopal Church. Ancient practice and the faith of the Apostolic Church are continued through the priesthood of the Episcopal Church. Clergymen serving in the Episcopal Church are on the Apostolic team, as it were. We hold to ancient practice so that we can absorb all the values of the past. However, we also emphasize democratic co-operation. The Episcopal vocation to the priesthood depends upon the co-operation of the minister and layman with God and with each other in the cause of Christ and His Church. Each has a responsibility before God in His Church. The priest is a commissioned co-operator; his office and work bring him esteem, but only as he is doing Christ's work and ministry in His name. In this regard every layman of the Episcopal Church has also a useful vocation before God. An elderly lady once said to me, "I am past usefulness." My answer to her was, "You are very helpful to me. Every Sunday you are always in your pew—a vital, wide-awake, interested worshipper. Also I often see you say a prayer for me. In both of these ways you are very helpful to me and to your Church." Because of our sacred ministry and the co-operative nature of the life of the Episcopal Church, we are indeed a link with the past and a hope for tomorrow.

Questions for Reflection or Discussion

1. Discuss the difference between a "disciple" and an "apostle."
2. Did Jesus Christ plan the ecclesiastical organization of the Church?
3. Why do we think bishops are so important?
4. How are Episcopal ministers priests in the One, Holy, Catholic, and Apostolic Church?
5. What is the special work of bishops?

6. Does the priest bestow absolution and blessing?
7. What is the difference between a deacon and a curate?
8. How do our ministers differ from those of the Presbyterians, Baptists, etc.? Is this important?

BOOKS FOR FURTHER READING

Butler, John V., and Pittenger, W. Norman, *What Is the Priesthood?* New York: Morehouse-Barlow Co., 1954.

10

The Government of the Episcopal Church

THE GOVERNMENT OF THE Episcopal Church must be considered against the entire sweep of the life and work of the Christian Church down through the centuries. The government of the Apostolic Church followed the example of Jewish tradition. Jewish government was vested in a Sanhedrin, which was a council of the elders. The Sanhedrin numbered approximately seventy members and had vested authority in civil and political affairs as well as in religious matters. It is interesting to note here that there is no word for "religion" in the Hebrew language. The reason for this is perhaps that for the Jew religion involves all of life. It is not strange therefore that the government of the early Church, led mostly by Jewish converts, would be vested in a council of the elders much like the Sanhedrin. Thus established, the government of general councils, which were councils of the Apostles and their successors, the bishops, persisted through many centuries. The general council was the highest Christian authority in all matters: faith, the Holy Scriptures, worship, and discipline.

With the rise of the power of the Bishop of Rome, climaxed by the crowning of Charlemagne by Pope Leo III, and the establishment of the Holy Roman Empire, the ancient prestige of Rome and the Bishop of Rome developed into government and order by papal supremacy. This was accomplished through many novelties and innovations introduced into primitive church discipline. The Pope was called Christ's Vicar and was endowed with vast temporal powers and wealth. From this he assumed authority as an autonomous ruler not only of his own kingdom but of many others also. The firm establishment of papal supremacy put an end to the apostolic-type ecumenical councils; they were simply not needed. The Council of Constance, which met in the early fifteenth century to deal with many of the cries for reformation, debated the question of authority in the Church and made a great declaration on the primal authority of general councils. Unfortunately Martin V, reigning at that time, ignored the council and it was later (1460) condemned by Pius II. This condemnation was the final death blow to conciliar government in the Church.

The Reformation brought about dramatic changes. On the continent Martin Luther developed the concept of a state-church protected by the prince of the state, and John Calvin taught a new theocracy which was based on a "town-meeting" of church elders. In England the reformed catholic state-church was established with the King as titular head. However, actually Parliament, the democratic body of the English government, assumed responsibility for the maintenance of the Church of England. In matters of faith, church councils, diocesan and provincial, speak for the Church. The Archbishop of Canterbury is the president of the councils of the Church. He is not the head of the Church of England, in the sense that the Pope is the head of the Church of Rome. He is also president of the meeting of the bishops of all Churches in communion with the Church of England. This great body is called the Anglican Communion and consists of more than forty million baptized members. The English Reformation produced within the Church a birth of democratic and representative government which is part of our rich heritage.

The title, "The Protestant Episcopal Church in the United States of America," gives a clue to the reformed and Apostolic character of our American Church. While in America the separation of Church and state is guaranteed, yet the Church and the state are partners in a great cause. The constitution of the Episcopal Church and that of our nation are much alike. This is not strange when we remember that some of the leading statesmen of the period were active churchmen, for example, George Washington, Benjamin Franklin, Alexander Hamilton, and many others. Indeed, Charles Pinckney and David Brearly, signers of the Federal Constitution of the new Republic, were both active in the General Conventions that formulated the constitution of the Protestant Episcopal Church. Such great Americans were among many who helped to insure the establishment of a democratic nation and Church as mutual partners in a new land. Both the United States Constitution and that of the Episcopal Church are built about a federal union of sovereign states (dioceses) each possessing independent and popular representative government. In the Church the constitution and canons together are a pattern for discipline in life and work. Canons are laws passed by General Convention to define the operation and function of ecclesiastical government under the constitution.

True to democratic tradition and the best interpretation of the federal system of government, the heart of the Church's government is the parish, the basic unit of the Church. An Episcopal parish is a self-supporting body incorporated by law, made up of contributors and voters according to a charter granted by the states. The fundamental, democratic parish meeting is much like a town meeting of New England assembled to hear reports and to act. It is the parish meeting which elects a vestry who, according to the law of the state, with the rector and wardens make up the legal local executive and trustee body. They are responsible for the parish fabric, for securing adequate income, and for the prudent expenditure of parish funds. It is the vestry's responsibility to elect a rector and serve as his council of advice. Wardens (Senior or Rector's and Junior or People's) are usually elected or selected to help with the over-all parish task. The rector of an Episcopal parish is assured of permanent tenure. He is by definition the spiritual leader and executive head responsible to the bishop of the diocese as well as to his parish meeting and vestry. A smaller parish aided in part or wholly by the diocese is called a mission and is under the bishop who is rector and a resident vicar who is in charge of the local work.

The large independent unit of the Episcopal Church's federal union is the diocese. A diocese is always a geographical division, a state or a part of a state including all the parishes and missions therein. The diocese is much like the autonomous state within the union of states. The bishop is much like the governor and the convention is much like a legislature. The diocesan convention is composed of clergy and lay delegates from every parish and mission. The voting for legislation is strictly democratic, with a special provision that the election of a bishop calls for a majority vote of both the clergy and the lay delegates voting separately. The bishop, whose title comes from the Greek word *episkopos,* meaning "overseer," is the executive and spiritual head of the diocese with constitutional safeguards, assisted by the executive council and other committees of the convention. He is the chief pastor of the diocese, with authority to ordain and confirm. A bishop coadjutor may be elected as an assistant bishop with the right of automatic succession upon the retirement or death of the diocesan bishop. A suffragan bishop may be elected as an assistant to the bishop without the right of succession. A missionary bishop is elected by the General Convention to be in charge of a missionary district.

The general central authority of the Episcopal Church is the General Convention. Like the general councils, this convention has authority in matters of faith, worship, and discipline. Like the bicameral Congress of the United States, it is composed of two houses, a House of Bishops and a House of Deputies constituted of four clergy and four lay delegates from each diocese. Both houses must concur to insure the passage of legislation. As an added constitutional safeguard, changes in the constitution must be referred to the dioceses before they are adopted by the following General Convention. The Presiding Bishop of the Episcopal Church is merely the president bishop. He also presides over the National Council consisting of bishops, clergy, and laymen whose task it is to insure the proper functioning of missions, Christian education, finance, and all other activities of the Church between conventions.

A standard Anglican organ, the province, has never become a really useful body in the Episcopal Church. We are organized into eight geographically aligned provinces composed of the dioceses in each area. Meetings are held annually except in a General Convention year. However, lacking legislative power, provincial meetings (synods) seem to accomplish very little.

Truly the government of the Episcopal Church is "of the people, by the people, for the people." It is a true democracy, thoroughly representative, depending upon the support and participation of *all* communicants. No clergy dictatorship by bishops or groups of clergy is possible, because of well documented safeguards. There are few lay "popes" (laymen who assume overbearing powers) in the Episcopal Church for the same reason. Each person has a proper role to play in the life and work of the Church. Each order, clergy and lay, functions with the other in harmony guided and upheld by constitutional and canonical discipline. Some people criticize the Episcopal Church government, saying that we are an ecclesiastical organization better suited to monarchy than to the United States. No criticism could be more wrong. The government of the Episcopal Church is an Apostolic pattern set within the framework of representative government. The concept of freedom basic to everything American is upheld vigorously by the Episcopal Church. Thus the Church shares with the United States popular, independent, federal, and representative government.

QUESTIONS FOR REFLECTION OR DISCUSSION

1. Discuss the reason for the close similarity of the constitution of the United States and the Episcopal Church.
2. How can the Episcopal Church be both Apostolic and democratic?
3. Compare the Episcopal system of church government with any other.
4. Do the laity have more voice in the government of the Episcopal Church than in the Roman Catholic and other communions?
5. Whose authority is higher, the rector's or the vestry's?
6. What is the authority of the bishop?
7. How is the General Convention like the United States Congress in composition, function, and authority?
8. Compare the offices of the Presiding Bishop and the Archbishop of Canterbury.

BOOKS FOR FURTHER READING

Addison, James T., *The Episcopal Church in the United States.* New York: Charles Scribner's Sons, 1951.

Dawley, Powel M., *The Episcopal Church and Its Work.* New York: Seabury Press, 1955.

Hodges, George, *The Episcopal Church.* New York: Morehouse-Barlow Co., 1938.

Wilson, Frank E., *What a Churchman Ought to Know.* New York: Morehouse-Barlow Co., 1943.

11

The Meaning of Christian Baptism

THE MEANING OF HOLY Baptism is certainly a most important and elemental matter for Christians to discuss. Holy Baptism is our initiation into the Church, into the divine society of God. Actually, in modern times, some wrong attitudes and practices have often caused it to be a mere social convention. When this happens Holy Baptism loses its true meaning. Many secular societies have much more impressive initiation rites than the average Christian rite. Is this because we make baptism too conventional and often perform it in isolation? The Church and all of its members are strengthened when the initiation rite is made impressive. Meaningful initiation should inspire us to say with deep pride, "I am a Christian." We can say this as enthusiastically as did the Roman citizen who said *Civis Romanus sum* ("I am a Roman citizen"). What an influence baptized members of the Church would be if they could say "I am a Christian" with just as much pride as the Roman of old.

To appreciate exactly what baptism can mean, picture a normal scene at the font with all its participants and drama. We who have been present at the font for the Sacrament of Holy Baptism will remember always that holy occasion. We remember well the hopes and prayers of those in attendance for the one initiated. We remember also that we are thereby reminded of the obligation of our own initiation into the Church.

Unfortunately, some abuses are attendant also at the font. Quite often baptism is thought of as a superstition or a charm. We hurry to "get it done" so that no "bad luck" will follow our children. How often are sponsors chosen for social and not religious reasons? Worst of all, some Christians have come to an unwritten but strange acceptance that baptism is to be a private rite without benefit of congregation. In a sense all of these are abuses of the Sacrament of Holy Baptism.

What is the teaching of the Church regarding Holy Baptism? What is required of those who are initiated into the divine society? The vows and promises of a Christian are twofold. First, baptism calls for a person's repentance, his turning away from sin with God's help. Second, baptism is a confession of faith, a turning toward God for His acceptance. The rewards of Holy Baptism are adoption into the family of God; salvation by His cleansing acceptance, and by the action of His grace within; and the promise of continued strength from God. All this is accomplished within the family of God and through the families of the Church. A very lovely illustration of the meaning of Holy Baptism was given by a little girl from Texas. When asked about her baptism she said, "I was a little maverick"—a maverick is a stray calf running around without a brand—"and then the minister put the Jesus mark on my forehead so when He or anyone else sees me they will know I am one of His children." This child will be one to say with pride, "I am a Christian."

The Church teaches that Holy Baptism is initiation into the Body of Christ, the family of God, and the Kingdom of Heaven. These words are not lightly used. Notice the position of the baptismal font. It stands at the church door, signifying initiation or entrance. Oftentimes it stands at the main door, or in the center of the church, signifying the importance of Holy Baptism within the divine society. One regret of many today is the absence of the congregation at the Sacrament of Holy Baptism. The Prayer Book advises (p. 273) that a private baptism is allowed only in exceptional cases. Otherwise the Holy Baptism is indicated "immediately after the Second Lesson at Morning or Evening Prayer, or at such other time as the Minister shall appoint."

Baptism is not a private rite and was never intended to be, but too many parents (and numerous other Christians) feel the church is not the place for a crying baby. We have separated his initiation to a time other than a service so that he won't disturb his parents or our dignity. How can we forget the fact that a congregation is challenged to receive this child into the fellowship of Christ? One of the most able bishops of the Church of England, the Right Reverend George Armitage Chase, retired Bishop of Ripon, told a clergy conference on Christian education about an unusual practice in administering the Sacrament of Holy Baptism in his diocese. When the minister comes to the words of reception everyone in the congregation sings out in unison: "We receive this child!" What a tremendous and impressive initiation rite this must be for all concerned. The importance of being received by the entire congregation ought to be considered by every family before plans for a baptism are made.

The Church teaches that the baptism of infants calls for understanding parents and sponsors. The Church demands that parents and sponsors take the vows of baptism on behalf of the child. In doing so they promise to help create and share the Christianization of the environment in which the child shall grow. This is a serious promise. Parents and sponsors should first of all be Christian members of the divine society themselves. How can you vow to renounce the devil, believe the Christian faith, and keep God's will and commandments unless you yourself are a practicing member of the redeemed community?

People often ask, "What about non-Episcopal sponsors?" If you read the Ministration of Holy Baptism in the Prayer Book, you will discover that, in addition to the above vows, the sponsors promise that the child will be brought to the bishop to be confirmed by him. Again this is a serious vow to ask just any friend to undertake. Surely they must understand what is implied herein before you ask them to be willing to accept and carry out this promise. Most of the bishops of the Church counsel that at least one of the sponsors should be an Episcopalian. All must be baptized Christians, but at least one should be an active communicant of the Episcopal Church.

Instruction in the meaning of baptism is important for both parents and sponsors. The Church must insist that all who have a share in this Sacrament should know more about it. Thus all will profit from an intelligible and responsible experience. Those of us who are active in church work hear this statement often: "Let a person choose for himself when he is old enough"; or, "Let a person come to the decision by himself—to influence him is unfair." Samuel Taylor Coleridge answered this argument for a friend by showing him a section of his garden covered with weeds. Said Coleridge: "This part has not yet come to horticultural decision by itself. It is unfair to prejudice the soil toward roses."

Let us examine the Sacrament itself. Here we should consult the Prayer Book, starting on page 273. The opening section includes the prayers, the lessons, the thanksgiving, and the examination containing the vows and promises that we have already discussed. Following the examination, the font is blessed and the actual baptism is consummated. Notice that the minister prays for the newly baptized child or person that he "may lead the rest of his life according to this beginning."

Critics are correct when they point out that infant baptism is not mentioned in the Bible as such. However, the Bible does record the baptism of entire families (see I Corinthians 1:16), and we can be certain that such baptism was the practice of the Apostles and early Fathers.

The baptism of an adult is far more impressive than that of infants, as indeed it should be. An adult stands up for himself and makes his confession of faith in Christ and his promise to follow Him. This confession is the heart and substance of adult initiation. The confirmation of a baptized adult should follow immediately. As a matter of fact, when anyone is baptized in the Episcopal Church, no matter what his age, that baptism presupposes his later confirmation. Both are a part of Christian initiation and thus are closely tied together within the Sacrament.

After the baptism itself comes the signing and receiving of the newest member of the Church. The priest says in the name of the congregation, "We receive this Child (Person) into the congregation of Christ's flock; and do sign him with the sign of the Cross, in token that hereafter he shall not be ashamed to confess the faith of Christ crucified, and manfully to fight under his banner, against sin, the world, and the devil; and to continue Christ's faithful soldier and servant unto his life's end." What a tremendous statement of the Christian cause! One of the great privileges of being an Army chaplain is the wearing of the cross. The symbol reminds all that in addition to wearing his country's uniform the chaplain is Christ's soldier and servant as well.

What then does baptism mean? What really happens? The inward and invisible grace of God is given in baptism. In some ways the value of a dollar bill is an illustration. The paper and ink in themselves are worthless outward symbols. It is the promise of the United States Government to stand behind it that gives the money its value. The grace of the baptismal font is in the promise of Jesus Christ to stand behind every disciple. The grace of baptism is God's strength supplied to His child in the indwelling of the Holy Spirit and the promise of our Lord and Master to walk with His child forever.

The story of Genesius, a third-century Roman actor who gave parodies on the Christian Sacraments, is appropriate here. While acting one day he said, "I have a great desire to be baptized." The miracle happened and he was given the grace of God. Genesius stopped in the middle of the play and said, "Something has happened to me." He was taken to the Emperor, who promised, "All you have to do is renounce this foolishness and live." The actor confessed his new faith with boldness: "There is but one God whose son Jesus Christ I adore and serve, to Him will I adhere though I suffer a thousand deaths."

What is the meaning of baptism? If you are a Christian you must know. You are marked with Christ's Cross. You are His soldier and servant unto your life's end.

QUESTIONS FOR REFLECTION OR DISCUSSION

1. Why baptize babies when they don't know what's happening to them?
2. Is the work of God's grace in Holy Baptism like magic?
3. Discuss the meaning of the outward sign of Holy Baptism.

4. Explain to your pagan friend the importance of your baptism.
5. Explain the meaning of the baptismal vows of repentance and faith.
6. Discuss the value of the presence of the parish congregation at Holy Baptism.
7. What is the *real* meaning of Holy Baptism for both parents and sponsors?
8. How can the administration of the Sacrament of Holy Baptism be made more impressive?

BOOKS FOR FURTHER READING

Coke, Henry C., III, *Why Baptize Babies?* Greenwich: Seabury Press (pamphlet).

Simcox, Carroll E., *Understanding the Sacraments* (Chapter III). New York: Morehouse-Barlow Co., 1956.

Southcott, Ernest W., *Receive This Child*. London: A. R. Mowbray & Co., 1951.

12

The Rite of Confirmation

OFTEN THOSE INTER-
ested in the Episcopal Church ask the question, "Why does
a Christian need confirmation?" In the interest of contributing to wider understanding on this subject, we must
define our terms. What is a Christian? A Christian is a baptized person, a child of God, a member of the Church, and
a follower of Jesus Christ. What is confirmation? The word
confirmation means to strengthen, to make strong or firm.

The relevance of confirmation to the Christian is immediately obvious. The Church uses its ancient rite of confirmation as a reminder and a renewal of Holy Baptism. The
outward sign of the laying on of hands in confirmation continues the action of baptism. However, the hands of the priest
who pours the water in the Sacrament of Holy Baptism give
way to the confirming hands of the bishops of the Church.
Still the inward grace is the same. It is the indwelling grace of
the Holy Spirit which is given to the Christian in Holy Baptism and confirmation. In both inward and divine acts our
souls are empowered to live the life and do the work of a
Christian. However, in confirmation, the vows and promises
of Holy Baptism already present in the individual are
strengthened by the continuing action of the Holy Spirit.

Thus confirmation is a more advanced gift of God's love and grace accepted by mature assent and attested to by the chief pastors of the Church.

In the early Church confirmation was a distinct and integral part of the rite of initiation. In the days of the Apostles the Church expected initiation to include a conversion experience, instruction, and then formal initiation through baptism and confirmation, which were often administered on the same day. From the font the baptized person went immediately to the Apostle for further instruction and the laying on of hands in confirmation. Thus fully initiated, he then received the Holy Communion at the altar as a full member of "the mystical Body of Christ." The primitive program of Christian initiation into the full life "in the holy fellowship" was meant to include baptism, Apostolic instruction, and the laying on of hands, and to culminate in the reception of the Holy Communion.

According to very early biblical records families asked, "How can our entire family be brought into the family of God?" To answer this the primitive Church arranged for infant baptism. Infant baptism was practiced with the provision that the child be instructed by the family in the faith and presented as early as possible for confirmation. This practice therefore assumed that both Holy Baptism and confirmation were included in the total family initiation program. Today in the Church an adult is directed by the Prayer Book rubrics to present himself immediately after baptism for confirmation. This is certainly a modern indication of the continuing relationship of both parts necessary to Christian initiation.

To answer more fully the question "Why does a Christian need confirmation?" we must answer the question "What happens in confirmation?"

First, in the rite of confirmation the Christian receives the necessary help from God to keep the promises of his baptism. The mystery of confirmation is that the Christian receives this strength by the continuing action of the Holy Spirit. Perhaps it is necessary to ask, "Who is the Holy Spirit?" How many of us understand the Nicene Creed, usually recited at the Holy Communion, where we name the Holy Spirit as "the Lord, and Giver of Life"? He is the "Giver of Life" because God is the Creator and Giver of all life. We see Him at Christmas as the "Giver of Life" in the form of Jesus Christ our Incarnate God through the Virgin Mary. We also see Him give new spiritual life in Holy Baptism. And as we observe His action through baptism, we may observe it also in confirmation.

The Holy Spirit is called "the Comforter" in the Bible and the Prayer Book. The modern word *comfort* connotes something easy and soft. The words actually mean "make strong" or "the Strengthener." The word *confirmation* therefore is actually what it connotes: "strength" because it is the Holy Spirit who is the divine Strengthener. In confirmation He comes to strengthen the soul of the Christian through the bishop in the laying on of hands. Thus the Holy Spirit imparts to God's child the "sevenfold gifts of the Spirit" by outward symbol and inspiration from the Church without and His grace within. Notice that these gifts include wisdom, the faculty of good judgment; understanding, the ability to discern, to know; counsel, the ability to make a right estimation; spiritual strength, the willingness to act through God's will; knowledge, true learning and its right use; godliness, the following of God's way; and holy fear, true reverence. These seven gifts of the Spirit are the gifts of God through His Holy Spirit in confirmation.

The effect of the action of the Holy Spirit in confirmation

is much like His work among the disciples at Pentecost. The Book of Acts describes the way He came to the humblest and the weakest of men, afraid and inept, and made them heroes and martyrs, sending them forth in Christ's name to win the world. Such was the faith of Marinus, a Roman soldier in the third century. When it was rumored that Marinus was a Christian, his commander called him in and told him he had been ready to give him a promotion, but now he would give him just three hours to renounce Christianity or die. The brave soldier went to the bishop of the Christian Church. We are grateful to him for recording the story. Marinus handed his sword to the bishop, who then put his hands on the head of the Roman soldier and confirmed him. Then, after he had received the Holy Communion, Marinus went forth to die. Such heroic faith is the work of the Holy Ghost in confirmation.

Second, in the rite of confirmation the Christian renews the baptismal obligation of the initiation Sacrament. It is here the Christian "comes of age," accepting for himself the full responsibilities of discipleship. The bishop asks each confirmand, "Do ye here . . . renew the solemn promise and vow . . . made . . . at your Baptism?" (Book of Common Prayer, p. 296). This is an important question, for since the basic promises of baptism are repentance and faith, and no one can truly live as a mature Christian without either, the Christian renews his plea for God's forgiveness and His new life. An English bishop has called confirmation "the Sacrament of Warriors." This surely is what it is. Baptized Christ's soldiers and servants, we are confirmed mature warriors and strengthened for adult service in the Christian army.

The bishop then asks, "Do ye promise to follow Jesus Christ as your Lord and Saviour?" Here is the real substance of the rite of confirmation: the public acknowledgment of Jesus Christ as Lord and Saviour. This is why confirmation is an important and necessary part of Christian initiation. Confirmation asks the Christian to make a grown-up giving of himself already given or dedicated to God in baptism. Perhaps the best story illustrating this appreciation of confirmation is the one about Queen Victoria, who received from the boy Maharajah of the Province of Punjab, the Kohinoor Diamond. Since this is one of the most beautiful diamonds in the world, it is well guarded in the Tower of London. In later years the Maharajah visited Queen Victoria and asked to see the diamond. Examining it carefully, he took it to a window for a closer look. Then he gave it back to her and quietly said: "Madam, I gave this present as a child too young to understand, to know its beauty and loveliness. I want to give it to you now as a man with all my heart, affection and gratitude." This is truly what a Christian does in confirmation. He offers to God the gift already given in baptism, which now, as a mature person, he presents to Christ in discipleship.

Finally, in the rite of confirmation the Christian is given access to the Holy Communion to nourish and sustain his soul. In the Prayer Book Offices of Instruction, the privilege of confirmation is discussed in the last question and answer on page 291. The answer is worth memorizing. "Our Lord provides the Sacrament of the . . . Holy Communion, for the continual strengthening and refreshing of my soul." What a beautiful expression of fact! Because of his mature initiation, the Christian receives the special benefit provided by our Lord for the faithful, the access to the table of the Lord's Supper. In the Holy Communion his gain is inner strength through direct contact with God our Saviour. How does this happen? The full answer will never be available. A lady was once asked, "What does the Holy Communion do for you?" Her answer is classic. "I really don't know," she said, "but I go up empty of good and come back full of God and strengthened to live a better life."

A very interesting story comes out of a Chinese Communist prison camp. A British (Anglican) chaplain had petitioned for permission to celebrate the Holy Communion. His captors at first allowed the service but finally refused with the comment, "Truly these have been eating that enchanted bread which casts a spell upon the soul." Pagans cannot understand the courage and strength available within the Holy Communion. Only the Christian knows the meaning of the words, "In thy presence is fulness of joy; at thy right hand there are pleasures for evermore" (Psalm 16:11).

Because of all these things it is obvious that a Christian does need confirmation, not only to find rich rewards in God's fellowship, but to pledge worthy discipleship to Him and to His Son Jesus Christ. Jenny Lind, one of the world's great vocalists, told this interesting story. It was in London in 1849. The concert was interrupted by a tattered man crying out, "Jenny, my Jenny!" With one accord the audience shouted, "Throw him out!" He was a pitiful sight indeed. "Let him speak," the singer said. And the man spoke: "With the birds, I was your first audience and it was I who predicted your greatness." Jenny Lind cried out, "Max Bronzden, my true and first friend. Come up to the stage." He knelt before her, but she said, "Rise, my friend, be no longer a vagabond but be a man worthy of my friendship." Max stood and said, "With God's help, I will!" This is exactly what happens in confirmation. Our Lord through His Apostles says, "Be no longer a child, be a man worthy of My discipleship." A Christian's answer to Him is, "With God's help, I will."

QUESTIONS FOR REFLECTION OR DISCUSSION

1. Answer the statement: "Confirmation is joining the Church."
2. Why must a newly baptized adult be presented for confirmation as soon as convenient?
3. Explain to your pagan friend what happens at your confirmation.
4. Why is confirmation at the hands of an Episcopal bishop necessary for one already confirmed by a minister of another communion?
5. Discuss: "Confirmation is both receiving new strength from God and pledging worthy discipleship to Christ."
6. What do you think the promise "to follow Jesus Christ as your Lord and Saviour" really implies?
7. Why do Christians need confirmation, anyway?
8. Discuss the admission to the Holy Communion as a benefit of confirmation.

BOOKS FOR FURTHER READING

Browne-Wilkinson, A. R., *The Prayer Book Way of Preparation for Confirmation*. London: Society for Promoting Christian Knowledge, 1952.

Diocese of New York, *Ready and Desirous*. Morehouse-Barlow, 1962.

Dix, Dom Gregory, *The Theology of Confirmation in Relation to Baptism*. Naperville, Ill.: Alec R. Allenson, Inc., 1953.

Little, A. W., *Reasons for Being a Churchman* (Chapter XX). New York: Morehouse-Barlow Co., rev. ed. 1905 (out of print but may be found in libraries).

Pardue, Austin, *The Eucharist and You*. Morehouse-Barlow, 1963.

13

The Holy Communion

Except for Jesus Christ her Lord and Saviour, nothing is more important to the Christian Church than the Sacraments. The Sacraments accepted by the universal Church are Holy Baptism and the Holy Communion, which were instituted and given by Jesus Christ, who also directed their use. These He made effective in the Church through His Incarnate and supernatural life, death, and resurrection. Holy Baptism guarantees the grace of the Son of God in us through the Holy Spirit's indwelling and is continued by the rite of confirmation. Holy Communion offers us the grace of the "continual remembrance of the sacrifice of the death of Christ" (Book of Common Prayer, p. 293). Without the Sacraments a person might say, "I am trying to be a Christian," or more weakly, "I hope to be a Christian." With the Sacraments a Christian asserts, "Holy Baptism made me a member of Christ and His Church, and Holy Communion with Christ continually strengthens and refreshes my soul."

The great and eternally binding commissions of Jesus Christ to His Church were: "Go ye into all the world, and preach the gospel [baptizing]" (St. Mark 16:15), and "Do this in remembrance of me" (St. Luke 22:19). True to our Lord's commission, the Church has baptized people as their earliest initiation into the Body of Christ. Also true to the Master's command, the Church celebrates the Holy Communion, which offers a continuing personal contact between Jesus Christ and each Christian. St. Paul was more emphatic when, in speaking of this point of personal communion with Christ, he wrote, "For as often as ye eat this bread, and drink this cup, ye do show the Lord's death till he come" (I Corinthians 11:26). The Apostle's counsel to his parish at Corinth is vital and helpful to the modern Church. The Holy Communion is indeed the best visual means of Christian education and evangelism.

In the Holy Communion we see the drama of the ages unfold. We are reminded of the Cross of Christ, where the Son of God actually fulfilled His prophecy within His words of institution, "this is my Body ... broken ... and my Blood ... shed" for the redemption of mankind. By some this action is labeled "unthinkable." Others call it "unexplainable." Yet by this act God's new covenant (testament) with man was effected. At the altar the drama continues as the Church offers to God the sacrifice of Christ with the same words "this is my Body . . . broken . . . my Blood . . . shed for thee." The action of the liturgy is threefold: first, the perfect offering of God's mighty act for man's redemption—the Cross of Christ; second, the less perfect offering of the Church which is itself no less than a mighty action of God's new covenant—the Body of Christ; third, the imperfect but necessary offering of each individual Christian, his "soul and body," to God in answer to His mighty acts for men in and through Jesus Christ. In the greatest act of worship the world has ever known, Christians celebrate God's divine offering in the offering of self with infinite thanksgiving.

Holy Communion is the Christian's strength because it is his sacred opportunity to obey our Lord's command and desire for His disciples. No other liturgical or corporate worship suggestion was given by our Lord except His command to baptize. The heart of the liturgy was given (instituted) by Christ as a part of the memorable Upper Room Passover celebration. Because of this fact it parallels the religious liturgy of the Old Testament. The Holy Communion is similar to the Jewish worship accompanying the evening meal, which includes the breaking of bread with thanksgiving and the offering to God of the cup of wine. It is most natural that the Apostolic Church obeyed Christ implicitly in its primitive worship.

In the Holy Communion, first-century disciples carried on a continuing and direct contact with Christ. St. Paul's testimony to this tells us much: "The cup of blessing which we bless, is it not the communion of the blood of Christ? The bread which we break, is it not the communion of the body of Christ?" (I Corinthians 10:16). Is it any wonder that early Christians defied death to meet Christ at His holy table? The Church down through the ages has continued to answer with joy the divine challenge of our Lord to meet Him at His table. Is it any wonder that the Lord's Supper or the "Holy Eucharist," as the Holy Communion is called by many catholic Christians, is the most sacred and universal form of Christian worship? The Holy Communion has always been the central act of corporate worship in the life of the Church— in the lives of Christians. Archbishop Fisher has counseled Anglicans regarding this great act of worship, "The Holy Communion is the center of a queen's coronation, and it can be the center of your life."

The centrality of the Sacrament in the life of the Episcopal Church is obvious to all observers. The Episcopal Church usually offers a celebration of the Holy Communion every Sunday morning and another at least one Sunday a month— in some parishes every Sunday—at a later hour. This schedule and weekday celebrations according to the Prayer Book use vary according to local customs. The extreme Protestant view of the Holy Communion is that it is a service which can be elected or not according to individual taste. The extreme Roman Catholic view is that the Mass is a weekly obligation for each Christian and that a penalty is connected with failure to attend. The Episcopal Church simply holds that, confronted with Christ's command and desire for His disciples to meet Him often at His holy feast, each Christian will want to make his Communion as regularly as possible.

The Holy Communion is the Christian's strength because it is the act of a disciple's highest stewardship. Two different but related words are used, one in describing, and the other in celebrating, the Holy Communion. The first is *Eucharist,* which means thanksgiving. The second is *Oblation,* which means offering. The Holy Communion is the Church's great, perfect feast of thanksgiving to God for His gift of salvation through Christ. In this offering of the sacrifice of Christ we find the drama of the perpetual "lifting up" of Christ to draw all men unto Himself. The Communion liturgy provides words which inspire our souls: "Who made there (by his one oblation of himself once offered) a full, perfect, and sufficient sacrifice, oblation, and satisfaction, for the sins of the whole world" (Book of Common Prayer, p. 80). At the Holy Table each Christian receives again and again God's redeeming and sustaining grace through the Holy Spirit for the healing and absolution so necessary to Christian living. It is well said that "we depend upon the Holy Communion as we depend upon our daily bread."

The Holy Communion is the act of a Christian's highest duty and obligation. The important word *oblation* must be understood by all. The Prayer Book leads us to say "And here we offer and present unto thee, O Lord, our selves, our souls and bodies, to be a reasonable, holy, and living sacrifice" (p.

81). This self-offering is necessary in order that we may achieve the new life in Christ otherwise so elusive. Each Christian is called upon to heed the invitation which summons us to make a positive offering and "repent you of your sins, [be] in love and charity with your neighbours, and intend to lead a new life" (p. 75). The duty and obligation of each Christian is to assist in the Holy Communion by our sincere offering of ourselves. Of course we are guilty of a serious sin if we receive the Sacrament but do not intend to make the essential self-offering.

The Holy Communion is the Christian's strength because it offers the faithful an opportunity for meeting Christ. The Church teaches that Jesus Christ is actually present in the Sacrament of the Altar. The real presence of our Lord in the Holy Communion is at once a mystery and a mastery of life. It is a mystery in every way. Indeed, it is a miracle. It might be compared to the miracle of the raising of Lazarus from the dead by our Lord (St. John 11:1-44). The question asked by Jesus of the family was, "Dost thou believe?" With Martha's answer, "Thou art the Son of God," the miracle of the raising of Lazarus was effected. The same miracle is accomplished by the Holy Communion. Christians are asked, "Dost thou believe?" With our corporate and unreserved confession of the deity of Jesus Christ, we are rewarded by the real presence of our Lord in the Eucharist.

Such a miracle of faith is also a mastery of life and is based upon our unbounded confidence in Christ Himself. As Christians we believe without question that Christ died and rose again, so we are empowered to believe that in the Holy Communion God the Holy Spirit imparts Christ's grace and presence. The Saviour's words of institution, "This *is* my Body . . . [and] Blood," are in themselves the key to the paradox of His presence within the symbols of His Holy Feast. The

Prayer Book expresses the Christian's personal conviction "that he may dwell in us, and we in him" (p. 81). By this dedication we seek the indwelling of Christ and His power that we may better live and serve Him in our day. The wonderful thing about the Holy Communion is that when we receive it sincerely, *He is in us.* Furthermore, when we leave the altar rail, *He goes with us.*

The need of the Church today is for its members to be strong and vocal in their faith. Someone has aptly said, "While we need to work for converts, we must remember that an important goal of the Church in our modern day is to make Christians more Christian." The celebration of our Lord's Supper is the Church's built-in opportunity to do just that. The Holy Communion is the best means whereby the Church can help Christians to understand their discipleship, aided by the strengthening and refreshing power of the Holy Spirit. At the altar Christians who are members of the Body of Christ are confronted with the present Jesus Christ. This meeting with our risen Saviour, Lord, and King cannot but inspire Christians to stronger faith, more powerful witness, and more noble living.

At the altar Christians meet as a true family. The Church is one in Christ. Each Christian is a member of Christ's Body and in intimate fellowship one with another. This is true Christian unity. At the altar Christians receive spiritual strength for daily living. With the other faithful communicants we take our place with the disciples of old, accepting both the great benefits and the responsibilities of personal communion with our Master. Prepared, worthy reception of the Holy Communion will give each Christian the inspiration and nourishment of the Spirit so necessary to the living of our day. The Holy Communion indeed is the strength of the Christian Church.

QUESTIONS FOR REFLECTION OR DISCUSSION

1. Why is the Holy Communion the distinctive act of Christian worship?
2. How is Christ present in the Holy Communion?
3. Explain the twofold offering of the Eucharist: the offering of the sacrifice of Christ, and the offering of ourselves.
4. In what way does the Holy Communion link past, present, and future?
5. Explain to your pagan friend what happens to a Christian at the altar.
6. How frequently ought the Christian to receive the Holy Communion?
7. What preparation is necessary for receiving the Holy Communion worthily?
8. Discuss the Holy Communion as a source of personal spiritual strength.

BOOKS FOR FURTHER READING

Bell, B. I., *The Altar and the World*. New York: Harper & Brothers, 1946.

Gifford, Frank D., *The Christian Way*. New York: Morehouse-Barlow Co., 1961.

Gilman, Phillips S., *In God's Presence*. New York: Morehouse-Barlow Co., 1935.

Shepherd, Massey H., Jr., *At All Times and In All Places*. New York: Seabury Press, 1953.

Sly, Harold, *A Lively Sacrifice*. London: A. R. Mowbray & Co., 1954.

14

The Book of Common Prayer

THE BOOK OF COMMON
Prayer is the most universally used book in the English
language with the exception of the Holy Bible. The Prayer
Book ranks with the Bible as exemplary of the best in classical
English literature. It antedates the King James Version and
has been called by scholars one of the finest writings in the
English tongue. While the Prayer Book is the accepted expression of the faith and worship of the English Church, it
was not simply a literary product of the English reformers.
The Prayer Book is the product of the spiritual aspirations
of mankind down through the centuries.

From the common feeling for worship developing through
many centuries of human religious progress, the Prayer Book
gathered and refined for English use the contributions of
many civilizations and religions. The Jewish religion contributed the Psalms and many other materials from the Old
Testament. Eastern Orthodox Churches contributed many
liturgical prayers and formularies. The Western Church contributed the Roman (Latin) liturgy, many of the Offices, and
also a great number of Collects. Because of this varied background, the Prayer Book is truly a product of a living society
expressing its living faith with inspired liturgy.

The enrichment of worship has always been a continuing

process and not a stagnating one. The great worship materials have abided and the mediocre have disappeared. An example of the growth and development of the materials of worship is seen in the accepted modern use of hymns as a regular feature of Christian worship. Critics often say, "I can't enjoy reading prayers out of a book," and "There is too much form in the Episcopal Church." The Prayer Book really provides common worship, the word *common* meaning "for all." The power of Prayer Book services which are admittedly for "all sorts and conditions of men" comes from a unity of congregation and minister. Indeed, the Prayer Book assumes a unity of all worshipping Christians, the present generation, those past, and those yet to come.

The Prayer Book eliminates the idea of the minister as a religious master of ceremonies. The extemporaneous non-liturgical approach to worship is often as formal as that of the Prayer Book. As a young man I listened to twenty-minute prayers from a Sunday school superintendent who covered the same ground in almost the same words every Sunday. To answer objections to Episcopal form or ceremony, I often refer to a cartoon which I saw picturing three men all dressed up for their lodge meeting, each one in his full regalia. The one was pictured saying to the others as they passed an Episcopal church, "I don't go for that Church, too much form in there."

Worship is made meaningful and effective because of the Book of Common Prayer. The idea of a book of worship is older than the Christian Church itself. Worship has always been regarded as the highest response of man to God. In the *Gloria in Excelsis* Christians acknowledge this truth, with the Jewish faithful: "Thou only art holy; thou only art the Lord." Jewish worship historically has been centered in the home and then secondarily in the Temple. However, the daily Offices of the Prayer Book contain the elements of prayer, praise, and instruction which have been carried over from Jewish worship.

Christian worship brought about a distinct change. As the Apostles and their followers continued "in breaking of bread, and in prayers" (Acts 2:42), the Christian Church early established the altar as the center of Christian worship. In the Holy Communion, the Church's great feast of thanksgiving for Jesus Christ, we have the unique action of Christian worship. The liturgy for this celebration developed through the Greek language into the Latin and then finally into the English, but withal the same basic structure has been constant. As Phillips Brooks said in discussing the agelong development of the liturgy, "Whatever the language . . . we know that where the bread is broken and the cup is blessed Christians are gathered together in Christ's name and He is in the midst of them."

The story of how we got our Prayer Book is a very interesting one and should be told and discussed by every Episcopal family. A lady who heard an Episcopal service on the radio said to her Episcopal neighbor, "If you can tell me who wrote the Prayer Book, I think I'll join the Episcopal Church." What would you have said? The truth is that *no one wrote* the Book of Common Prayer. It was compiled by bishops of the Church of England in consultation with learned doctors and theologians and led by Archbishop Cranmer. Thomas Cranmer was the outstanding figure in the English Reformation. Guided by his masterful pen, the restoration of ancient worship materials throughout the Prayer Book was accomplished. The Holy Bible of course contributed the vast majority of the materials used. Also, the "Godly and decent order of the Ancient Fathers" was consulted and appropriated. The Prayer Book contains many prayers from the Apostles and their successors and heirs down through the course of church history. It must be remembered that the liturgy and other offices taken from the Roman rite had been used in the Church of England many centuries before the printing of the Prayer Book. From these much of the remainder of the material was taken.

The first English Prayer Book was used on Whitsunday, 1549, during the reign of King Edward VI. It was described as "a form of worship founded upon practical doctrines of the early Church, free from error and over-elaboration." The Prayer Book was revised several times in the years to follow: 1552, 1559, and 1604, until the standard Book of Common Prayer was established by a revision in 1662. Roman and Puritan criticism and persecution were almost constant in the years between 1549 and 1662, but they were overcome by the efforts of both nation and Church. One of the Deans of Canterbury, commenting upon this dual attack on the Prayer Book, remarked, "Every Pope is an open schismatic and every schismatic is a secret pope." The Prayer Book helped the Church of England to remain free, constant, and a witness to Christ and to His mission down through the centuries.

Both Roman and Puritan worship extremes illustrate some failures in the field of common worship. The failure of common worship in lands where Roman (Latin) services were maintained and where no prayer book in the language of the people was developed, has been a cause of great concern in the Roman Catholic Church over the years. The liturgical movement, one aim of which is to restore common worship to the people in their own tongue, is their late answer to this problem. The failure of Protestant free extemporaneous worship to provide "common worship" has also been answered in the last few years by a movement toward prayer-book type worship. There are only a few major communions which today do not have a book of worship similar or parallel to the Prayer Book.

The American Church established its own Book of Common Prayer following the American Revolution, "according to the use of the Protestant Episcopal Church in the United States of America." However, the Prayer Book Preface assured that the doctrine, discipline, and worship of the Church was to remain unchanged. In 1789 the revised American Prayer Book was published. This revision deleted reference to royalty and made other changes congruous with the revolutionary and new-land spirit. The new Prayer Book contained an outstanding contribution from the Episcopal Church of Scotland, the matchless Prayer of Consecration from the Scottish liturgy. Revisions in 1892 and 1928 continued to bring the Prayer Book up to date with a growing America. However, no major change in basic universal "common" worship was ever contemplated or accomplished. The Book of Common Prayer is today published in more than 150 different languages and may be found in current use on every continent and in almost every country around the world.

The Prayer Book speaks to all of life. It is indeed five books in one. The title page gives a clue: "The Book of Common Prayer and Administration of the Sacraments and Other Rites and Ceremonies of the Church"; together with the Psalter and the Ordinal. While common prayer is obvious throughout this great book, Morning Prayer, Evening Prayer, the Litany, and other corporate, family, and individual materials especially encourage active lay use and participation. Indeed, it is important to the Prayer Book services of the Church that laymen participate enthusiastically. Episcopal worship contains that blending of prayer, praise, and instruction so necessary to the growth of Christians. For this reason especially the Psalter has always been most important to the Church. The Psalms still hold a high and original place among the great songs of our worship.

The major Sacraments administered in the Episcopal Church are Holy Baptism and Holy Communion, the universal Sacraments of the Church instituted by Christ Himself and commended by Him to His Church. The initiation Sacrament calls upon the sponsor or person being baptized to repent and have faith and thus be made a member of Christ's Church. The Holy Eucharist calls each communicant to join in Christ's sacrificial offering and thankfully offer himself to God in "repentance, love, charity, and new life." The Sacraments are the very breath and strength of the Christian.

Other sacramental rites, often called the minor Sacraments, include the Order of Confirmation (pp. 296-299); the Solemnization of Matrimony (pp. 300-304); Unction of the Sick (p. 320); Penance, which is written into every service but is especially provided for in the Visitation and Communion of the Sick (pp. 313 and 323) ; and Holy Orders, the "Form of Making, Ordaining, and Consecrating Bishops, Priests, and Deacons" (pp. 529-562). The first four rites speak to the special areas and needs in the life of a Christian where the Church provides God's special grace and blessing. The Ordinal insures that, as members of a local church, Episcopalians are one with the Apostles and thus with the Church of God into which Episcopal clergy are ordained by the reception of the Holy Spirit.

Other rites and ceremonies are provided by the Church in the Book of Common Prayer. They include the great Pastoral Offices: the Offices of Instruction (pp. 283-295); the Thanksgiving of Women after Child-birth, a little used but magnificent Office (pp. 305-307); the Visitation of the Sick (pp. 308-320); the Communion of the Sick (pp. 321-323); and the Burial of the Dead (pp. 324-342). In the Pastoral Offices the

Prayer Book serves the many needs of churchmen and provides them with an ever present opportunity to give testimony to their faith, even in death. The Prayer Book also provides a Form for the Consecration of a Church or Chapel (pp. 563-568), an Office of Institution of Ministers into Parishes or Churches (pp. 569-574), and Forms of Prayer to be used in Families (pp. 587-593).

The practical values of the Prayer Book for today are five-fold:

1. *The Prayer Book emphasizes God, not one's self nor the minister.* We may go to church thinking of ourselves, but the Prayer Book centers our thoughts on God.
2. *The Prayer Book, following the Church Year, lends change and variety to worship.* Advent, Christmas, Epiphany, Lent, Easter, Ascension, Whitsunday, and Trinity—all are potent teachers of the Gospel and witnesses to our Lord.
3. *The Prayer Book maintains biblical truth and the faith of the Church.* One who attends church regularly is exposed to thorough and systematic Bible reading as well as the continual recitation of the Church's faith.
4. *The Prayer Book is a universal book.* Forty million Anglicans find it their common expression of faith and worship. An American at church in Australia would be able to follow the service as though he were at home.
5. *The Prayer Book is an ageless book.* It looks backward and it looks forward. The Prayer Book is catholic, evangelical, apostolic, and ecumenical.

The Episcopal Church has room in its worship for all because of the Prayer Book. Louis Bouyer, a Roman Catholic priest, has said that the Prayer Book presents "not only one of the most impressive, but also one of the purest forms of

Christian Common Prayer to be found in the world." Roman Catholics, Protestants, and even non-Christians can find elements in it which are comfortable and inspiring. The Prayer Book helps all who would use it to worship God "in the beauty of holiness and the holiness of beauty."

QUESTIONS FOR REFLECTION OR DISCUSSION

1. Why does the Church emphasize *corporate* worship?
2. Answer: "I can't enjoy prayers out of a book."
3. What are the advantages of Prayer Book worship over any other?
4. Why do the Psalms continue to aid corporate worship?
5. What is the value of ceremonial in the Church's worship?
6. Answer: "I can worship God anywhere as well as in church."
7. Explain to a non-Episcopalian how we got our Prayer Book.
8. How may the Prayer Book be used for individual and family prayers as well as in corporate worship?

BOOKS FOR FURTHER READING

Boss, Nelson R., *The Prayer Book Reason Why*. New York: Morehouse-Barlow Co., 1942.

Burgess, Francis G., *The Romance of the Book of Common Prayer*. New York: Morehouse-Barlow Co., 1930.

Parsons, Edward L., and Jones, Bayard H., *The American Prayer Book*. New York: Charles Scribner's Sons, 1937.

Pell, Walden, and Dawley, Powel M., *The Religion of the Prayer Book*. New York: Morehouse-Barlow Co., rev. ed. 1950.

Shepherd, Massey H., Jr., *The Oxford American Prayer Book Commentary*. New York: Oxford University Press, 1950.

Shepherd, Massey H., Jr., *The Worship of the Church*. New York: Seabury Press, 1952.

15

The Prayer Book and the Life of a Christian

THE COMPREHENSIVENESS of the Book of Common Prayer is astounding. No area of life escapes its concern and coverage. It might well be called the "Prayer Book of the Christian Family," for it provides for the worship of each individual and his natural family. In addition to the regular Prayer Book services—the choir Offices, the Liturgy, the Ordinal, and the Psalter—there is a short section sometimes called the "Occasional Services," or the "Services of the Christian Life." This is a pastoral section that appeals to us because it appeals to our common experiences and the events in our lives when we need help from God. It follows in a broad way the sequences of the events in the life of a Christian, noting his progress from stage to stage.

The Occasional Services section begins with Christian initiation, Holy Baptism and Confirmation, already discussed in Chapters 11 and 12 of this book. It also contains the Visitation and the Communion of the Sick, discussed in Chapter 22, "The Healing Ministry of the Church."

The Prayer Book speaks to five other great events or stages in the Christian life as guided and counseled by the Church: Christian education, the Christian home, Christian marriage, Christian repentance, and Christian burial.

Christian education is highlighted in the Prayer Book Offices of Instruction (pp. 283-295) and the Catechism (pp. 577-583). The Offices of Instruction of course contain the Catechism, plus additional materials on the Church, the ministry, and the Holy Communion, with prayers and versicles for use in either the Church School or the home.

The Christian home and family are not forgotten in the Prayer Book. The vows of the sponsors (and parents) in Holy Baptism (pp. 276-277) reveal the basic responsibility of the Christian home in the spiritual growth and development of the child's Christian life. The helpful Family Prayer section in the Prayer Book (pp. 587-600) is a mighty resource for the Christian family. A lovely short service, the Thanksgiving of Women after Child-birth (pp. 305-307), is also available for appropriate use.

Christian marriage is given an impressive beginning in the beautiful and much copied Prayer Book Solemnization of Matrimony (pp. 300-304) and the appropriate propers (pp. 267-268) to be used in the Holy Communion. The Prayer Book also provides for the publishing (the announcing) of the Banns (a signed intention) of marriage (p. 304, last rubric). There are many who feel that a return to the reading of the Banns might prevent hasty marriages.

The opportunity for Christian repentance is provided in every Prayer Book service. The Invitation in the Holy Communion (p. 75), the Exhortations to Confession in Morning and Evening Prayer (pp. 5-6 and 23) and the rubrics of the Visitation and Communion of the Sick (pp. 313 and 323) all counsel the Christian to true repentance.

The Order for the Burial of the Dead (pp. 324-342) and the appropriate propers for the Holy Communion (pp. 268-269) are the Prayer Book's provision for Christian burial. This is a service much copied by other Christian communions, mainly because it is recognized as a service of Christian hope and joy.

Perhaps a more careful examination of each one of these experiences and events as it is touched on in the several Prayer Book areas will prove profitable, for in a very real sense they do note the progress of the Christian through his life as led by his Church.

Christian education by definition is a system of teaching set in the framework of the Christian faith. The Deuteronomic Law commanded us to "teach diligently . . . thy children" (Deuteronomy 6:7). The Church is also committed to pass her heritage of revelation and experience to future generations. Telling the story of how God has dealt with His people in the environment of the Community of God is one of the prime tasks of Christ's Church.

Christian education is not "training in religion." Animals are "trained"; human beings are educated. The word *educate* means to "lead forth." This task the Christian Church accepts and calls upon each home to share.

Modern theories tell us that we educate not just part of a person—we educate the whole person: his physical, mental, and spiritual attributes. It is interesting to note that there is such a trinity in each one of us. To educate just the physical (the body) alone in the art of mere living is to chance producing a delinquent. To educate the mental (the mind) alone in the art of thinking only is to chance making a clever rascal. To add the spiritual (the soul), however, chances nothing, for with all three attributes contributing, the product is a living soul, the main quality of the good individual and thus of the good society.

That the Christian home is prerequisite to effective Christian education is evidenced in the vows of baptism. Herein the home's responsibility is set forth most definitively. Christians are to provide a Christian atmosphere and environment for the person who is baptized. Thus Christian living is revealed as something which is experienced as well as taught. But we must teach something specific, since the vows of baptism require us to teach "the Creed, the Lord's Prayer, and the Ten Commandments, and all other things which a Christian ought to know and believe to his soul's health" (Book of Common Prayer, p. 277). This very strict burden for Christian education in the home has been avoided in the last number of years with unfortunate consequences.

The Christian home is the gateway to the Church. It was, and continues to be, the basic Christian unit. The most precious church usage was begun in a home—the Lord's Supper, which was celebrated first in the upper room in the home of St. Mark. The mutual and adhesive concerns of both home and Church are love, which is the dynamo of both; confidence, which, as John Wesley put it, is "taking God at His word"; and service, which is a natural outcome of love and confidence.

There are many who believe that the home is the original, and some say the only, teaching unit. As one modern slogan aptly puts it, Christian faith is more often caught than taught. The modern need is for fathers who will say with Joshua, "Choose you this day whom ye will serve . . . but as for me and my house, we will serve the Lord" (Joshua 24:15).

The Christian home, of course, must be undergirded by the Church. The Church provides help for the home through its ministry, material, and motivation. Many families are looking for help at this point. The Church and the Prayer Book provide an answer to their cry, "What shall we do?"

The Prayer Book gives help toward a life of personal and family prayer; and to consult the several sections of the Prayer Book for these helps will prove most rewarding.

As indicated above, the Prayer Book gives help for basic family instruction in the faith. To use the Offices of Instruction at home will prove to be a rich beginning. Finally, the Prayer Book and the Church give direction to the cause of missionary concern and interest. The home undergirded, inspired, and motivated by the Church will live as a Christian cell in a pagan community.

Christian marriage as provided for in the Prayer Book Solemnization of Matrimony is primarily the witnessed union of two baptized Christians. It was once two separate services, both of which are recognizable in the modern service. The first part is the betrothal service, including all the materials up to the point at which the priest says, "Who giveth this woman to be married to this man?" The second part is the nuptial service, which may most happily include the Holy Communion. The nuptial Communion will assist the couple to realize the meaning of the petition in the appointed Collect: ". . . that they, seeking first thy kingdom and thy righteousness, may obtain the manifold blessings of thy grace" (Book of Common Prayer, p. 267). A relic of the nuptial Communion is the approach of the couple to the altar for the final vows, the prayers, and the blessing.

The symbolism of Holy Matrimony is most important and interesting. The ring, of course, is the major symbol. It is a perfect circle, speaking of unending, perfect love. The ring is often made of gold, indicating purity. The couple themselves are the ministers of the service, consecrated by the exchange of rings and the vow, "With this Ring I thee wed: In the Name of the Father, and of the Son, and of the Holy Ghost. Amen." Thus it may be said that the couple marry themselves, the priest solemnizes the wedding, and the Church is the witness.

Two other symbols are present. The first is the symbol of the mystical union between Christ and His Church. The qualities existing between Christ and His Body, the Church, are love, respect, and spiritual unity. A marriage built on these qualities will be happy indeed! The second is the symbol of the Church giving the bride to the groom. The father gives the bride's hand to the priest, who then gives her hand to the groom. This symbol makes clear the partnership of God in the estate of matrimony.

Christian repentance is a neglected teaching in modern Christendom in spite of the testimony of the Bible and the Book of Common Prayer. The Bible is very forceful in its teaching. St. John writes in his first Epistle: "If we say that we have no sin, we deceive ourselves, and the truth is not in us" (I John 1:8). The Prayer Book is most definite in the invitation to confession in the Holy Communion: "Ye who do truly and earnestly repent . . . and intend to lead a new life . . . make your humble confession . . ." (p. 75).

Three steps are generally acknowledged to lead to true and earnest repentance. The first is contrition: the acknowledgment of sin before God. Of course, contrition must be more than merely an emotion, a feeling; it must take the form of some Godward motion. The second step is confession. Confession is actually the expression of contrition. Someone has compared the relationship of contrition and confession to an alarm clock. Contrition is setting the clock and perhaps hearing it go off, but confession is getting up to follow through on the next step. The Church does provide for sacramental or auricular confession when desired by a penitent. The oft-quoted rule regarding such confession in the Episcopal Church is, "All may, some should, none must."

The third step of Christian repentance is amendment, following forgiveness and absolution through Christ and His Church. St. John assures us that "if we confess our sins, he is faithful and just to forgive us our sins" (I John 1:9). Usually we must add, however, restoration and penance, when it is necessary, before we find true amendment of life. This area of the Christian life cannot be taken lightly. Indeed, Thomas Carlyle has said, "Of all acts, is not repentance the most divine? The deadliest sin . . . consciousness of no sin—that is death."

Christian burial is the final event of the Christian's life. Like the other deepest moments of his life, baptism, confirmation, Holy Communion, and matrimony, the final act of worship is performed for him before God's altar in the Burial Office. Here is a benediction for the deceased along with an act of witness for the living to his hope of eternal life, which he has in Jesus Christ. The Pauline lessons appointed for the Burial Office are among the most beautiful of all the New Testament passages. They are matched by the later prayer of the Office urging that we be not "sorry, as men without hope, for those who sleep in him" (p. 335). The Church is the best, if not the only place for the service of Christian burial. It is a Christian's final opportunity to witness.

The Burial Office is divided into four parts: the procession with praise in sentences and psalms; the lessons, which have been described as the most magnificent passages in Holy Scripture because they apply not only to death but also to life; the prayers, which could of course include the Holy Communion; and the service at the grave where we join in singing "Blessed are the dead who die in the Lord . . ." (p. 333). The celebration of the Holy Communion at the Burial of the Dead is most appropriate, for we remember that it is the mighty resurrection of Jesus Christ from the dead which secures the Christian's resurrection. The liturgy calls us to render unto God "most hearty thanks for the innumerable benefits procured unto us by the same" (p. 81).

The question is raised: "How about prayers for the dead?" Episcopalians believe such prayers to be the ordinary custom of the Church, short of the extremes of Rome. The Prayer for the Whole State of Christ's Church in the Holy Communion includes a portion "for all thy servants departed this life in thy faith and fear; beseeching thee to grant them continual growth in thy love and service" (pp. 74-75).

The prayer in the Burial Office petitions "that he may go from strength to strength, in the life of perfect service, in thy heavenly kingdom" (p. 332). Believing in the Communion of Saints—that great and eternal fellowship of those in Paradise and on earth—we pray "that with them we may be partakers of thy heavenly kingdom" (p. 75).

The Prayer Book gives a true picture of the relationship of the Church to the Christian and his family at every point in his life, from his birth to the grave, as nurtured in the family of God. Baptized God's child and confirmed a mature Christian in the Spirit-filled Church, he grows in the faith through Christian education and a Church-motivated family, and he is inspired to hold and witness to his faith. He is blessed in marriage before God's altar. He is forgiven in repentance as the Church confronts him with the Gospel, and with the way of true penitence. Finally, even in death a Christian will witness to triumphant faith and confidence in Christ's triumph and resurrection and the uniquely Christian doctrine of life eternal.

The Prayer Book provides for universal sharing of the great Christian heritage, the faith which makes for a good life in Christ at every stage of the Christian's life on earth and beyond.

QUESTIONS FOR REFLECTION OR DISCUSSION

1. How do you think the Catechism can be used with profit by a Christian family in the teaching of children?
2. What are some of the ways the Church can assist the Christian home and the home assist the Church in doing a better job of Christian education?
3. Justify the statement that in the Prayer Book Solemnization of Matrimony the couple are the "ministers" of the service.
4. Which of the several symbols of Christian marriage seems most significant to you? Why?
5. Why does the Prayer Book provide an opportunity for confession in every service?
6. How would you explain to your neighbor the opportunity for auricular confession afforded by the Episcopal Church?
7. Comment on the trend to "funeral parlor" burial services in the light of the teaching of this chapter.
8. Discuss the relation of All Saints' Day and the Church's custom of prayers for the dead.

BOOKS FOR FURTHER READING

Barrett, Thomas V., *The Christian Family*. New York: Morehouse-Barlow Co., 1958.

Bayne, Stephen F., *Christian Living*. New York: Seabury Press, 1957.

Murray, John, *The Daily Life of the Christian*. Naperville, Ill.: Alec R. Allenson, Inc., 1956.

Urwin, E. C., *Religion and the Common Man*. London: Student Christian Movement Press, 1951.

Williams, J. G., *God and the Human Family*. New York: Seabury Press, 1958.

16

The Church Year

To a generation of persons familiar with Cinemascope, Todd-A-O, and Vistavision, the cyclorama of the Prayer Book Church Year may not seem spectacular at first glance. However, a serious study of it reveals a glorious worship-symphony of color, music, literature, and devotion, experienced by the Episcopal Church each year. Further study reveals the dramatic Person who is the main theme and hero of this magnificent spectacle: Jesus Christ.

There is little new, not even for the Christian Church, about a full year's pattern for worship. Christian worship has deep and appropriate backgrounds in Jewish worship. The preacher of Ecclesiastes described such a pattern: "To every thing there is a season, and a time" (3:1). Sabbath worship and three annual festivals, along with special feasts, made up the Jewish worship year. The festivals which corresponded to changes in the natural year were Passover, celebrated for eight days following the spring equinox (about March 21st); Pentecost, an eight-day holiday coming fifty days later and celebrating the first harvest thanksgiving; and Tabernacles (Booths), an eight-day holiday coming in the fall and celebrating the last harvest. The special feasts were New Year, Day of Atonement, Dedication, and Purim, each one arranged to fit a special spot in the Jewish calendar year.

The early Christian Church followed the Jewish calendar. This is made plain in the Acts of the Apostles (20:16), where the effort of St. Paul to be at Jerusalem for Pentecost is noted. The first Christian departure from the Jewish calendar was in the proclamation of Sunday, the day of Christ's resurrection, as the Church's holy day. This set a new pattern in the calendars of the world, but for the Christian the first day was his day of worship. This new day of worship was not to be the Old Testament Sabbath, but rather a Christian feast with no list of special restrictions.

The development of the Christian Church calendar is a long and interesting story, beginning with the first calendar called the Julian calendar, and ending with the adoption by the Western Church of the calendar of Gregory. The Christian calendar is based on Easter, which is the first Sunday after the first full moon after the spring equinox (which is, as we noted above, about March 21st). All the dating of the Christian calendar centers about the life of Christ. The very division between antiquity and the Christian age was made in His honor. B.C. means "before Christ" and A.D. means *anno Domini,* literally, "in the year of our Lord."

The Church Year is the opportunity provided by Mother Church for Christians to respond to many changes and varieties in natural life with variety and change of pace in worship. As in Jewish worship, some Christian feasts are related to Nature's seasons. However, our worship is not based on the sun, the fields, or even the harvest, but on Jesus Christ, the Son of God.

In some ways the Church Year is an expanded Creed. In it and through its lessons we go with our Lord through His earthly life. We see the Star of Bethlehem and hear the angels sing their message of peace and love at Christmastide. We walk the streets of Nazareth with Christ as a little boy.

We stop in the carpenter shop of Joseph where our Lord was an able assistant. In Galilee and elsewhere we watch the sick healed, the troubled helped, and the sinners forgiven. We share the temptation and prayer of the wilderness with our Lord during Lent. We experience the bitter anguish of Holy Week as we enter Jerusalem and share each eventful day. On Maundy Thursday we are refreshed as we celebrate the Holy Communion in remembrance of Him. On Good Friday we follow the Via Dolorosa prayerfully to Calvary. We become witnesses to His glorious resurrection on Easter. Finally, forty days later we see Him ascend.

> The way before us lies
> Replete with signs—through which in fixed career
> As through a Zodiac, moves the ritual year
> Of England's Church—stupendous mysteries!
> Which whoso travels in her bosom, eyes
> As he approaches them with silent cheer.[1]

The Prayer Book Church Year has provided "a season and a time" for everything relevant to the Christian's faith and life.

There are three separate sections of the Christian Year: first, the periods and events specifically related to Jesus; second, the Sundays after Trinity; and third, the saints' days and holy days.

The first section of the Prayer Book Church Year revolves about the Christmas and Easter festivals with their preparatory fasts and other related seasons. The feasts of Christmas and Epiphany are fixed, which means that they occur on the same date every year. The Advent season, including the four Sundays before Christmas, brings in the Church's New Year. Its color is violet because it stresses the devotional prepara-

---

[1] Source unknown.

tion necessary for a Christian's worthy reception of the coming Christ. Its major Collect petitions "that we may cast away the works of darkness, and put upon us the armour of light" (Book of Common Prayer, p. 90).

Christmas is one of the two great feasts of the Christian Church. It honors the Incarnation of our Lord. The feast of the Nativity is set annually for December 25th. Its color is festival white. In worship, carols, and the Holy Communion we join with the saints of heaven and earth in singing "O come, let us adore him" (No. 12, The Hymnal 1940).

Each year on January 6th, the feast of the Epiphany, we commemorate the visit of the Magi to the Child Jesus. The Epiphany is the festival celebrating God's manifestation of His Son to the Gentiles. Its missionary message proclaims that Christ is Saviour of all mankind and the Light of the whole world. The color of the feast of the Epiphany is white. Epiphanytide, or the Epiphany season, has green for its color. The season extends from the Epiphany to Septuagesima Sunday and may include from one to six Sundays, depending on the date of Easter.

Easter is the hub of a large part of this first section. As we have observed earlier, the date of Easter is variable; it can be as early as March 22nd, or as late as April 25th. The date of Easter determines the dates of all the related feasts and fasts, from Septuagesima through Trinity Sunday, and it also determines the number of Sundays after Epiphany and after Trinity.

Three Sundays before Lent, Septuagesima (70th), Sexagesima (60th), and Quinquagesima (50th), are so named because they are approximately that many days before Easter. This brief period is often called Pre-Lent and its color is violet.

Lent begins with Ash Wednesday, which is forty weekdays before Easter (Sundays are always feast days). The color of Lent (as was that of Advent) is violet because it is a season of penitential preparation to be "kept" by all. The Prayer Book Collect for Ash Wednesday (p. 124), which petitions God to "create and make in us new and contrite hearts," is a symbol of the necessary Christian discipline of our choice between Christ and the world.

Passiontide includes the last two weeks of Lent—Passion Week and Holy Week—during which the Church commemorates her Lord's "blessed passion and precious death." Passion Sunday, the Fifth Sunday in Lent, received its name from the Gospel which tells of the beginning of Christ's Passion (suffering) with the stoning threat in the Temple.

Holy Week begins with Palm Sunday, an unusual day on which churches are decorated with a most eloquent decoration: the palms recalling those which were strewn in the way of the victorious Christ. Included in Holy Week are Maundy Thursday and Good Friday. Maundy (a corruption of the Latin word for "command") Thursday is the day on which our Lord instituted the Holy Communion with His Apostles in the Upper Room. The color for Maundy Thursday when the Holy Communion is celebrated is white. Good Friday is without doubt the most universally observed sacred fast day of the Christian Year. It commemorates the death of our Lord upon Calvary's Cross. The color of Good Friday obviously is black. Also part of Holy Week is the traditional Easter Even Christian baptism preparatory to Apostolic confirmation and the festival Holy Communion of Easter.

Easter, honoring the Resurrection of our Lord, ranks with Christmas as the greatest of the Christian festivals. Each year it comes as a springtime burst of new life and light. The color of Eastertide is white. In worship and the Holy Communion, we celebrate this great feast with world-wide Christendom when we sing our triumphant testimony, "Jesus Christ is risen today, Alleluia" (No. 85, The Hymnal 1940).

The Ascension of our Lord came forty days after Easter following a number of important post-Easter appearances to His Apostles. The color of this most important festival is white. The Ascension is so important to the Church because it is the final mighty work of God in His Son Jesus Christ. With the ages we join in singing "Hail the day that sees him rise" (No. 104, The Hymnal 1940).

Whitsunday, or Pentecost, comes fifty days after Easter and honors the coming of God the Holy Spirit to the Church of the Apostles. The color of Pentecost is red, signifying the fire which the Church described as the symbol of the Holy Spirit's descent and birth of the Church. Red is also used for the days of saints who were martyrs, signifying the inspiration of the Apostles by the Holy Spirit to triumphant witness even unto death.

Trinity Sunday is the Sunday following Whitsunday. Anglican-inspired, this festival honors the Holy Trinity, a dogma essential to the Christian faith. The color used on Trinity Sunday is white.

The second section of the Prayer Book Church Year includes all the Sundays after Trinity. This is a large section sometimes including more than half the Sundays of the calendar year. The color of the Trinity season is green. It is a most obvious color, signifying the new life and growth that is all about in the spring, summer, and early fall. The celebration of the relation of the Triune God to the Church, which was begun on Trinity Sunday, is continued throughout the Trinity season as Mother Church supplies for each Christian new life and growth through the power of the Holy Spirit.

The third section of the Prayer Book includes numerous saints' days and holy days. All Saints' Day falls on November first and commemorates "all the saints, who from their labors rest" (No. 126, The Hymnal 1940). Its color is festival white. The feasts of other saints in the Prayer Book Church Year are celebrated on the days ascribed either to their birth or to their martyrdom or death. The Prayer Book offers prayers only for those saints who were part of the New Testament record. It thus avoids the Roman Catholic multiplicity which includes many heroes of legendary nature. It keeps before our minds the good example and the faithful life of the Church's saints and martyrs.

Ember days are appointed at the four seasons, three days during Advent, Lent, and Pentecost, and in September. These days turn our minds to a special interest in the sacred ministry. The three days before Ascension Day are appointed as Rogation Days, on which we pray for a fruitful earth and a good harvest. Thanksgiving and Independence Day are American holidays which the Episcopal Church celebrates. They illustrate the close connection of faith and life under the guidance of Almighty God.

The Table of Fasts on page li of the Prayer Book is the basic guide for individual acts of devotion and preparation. It lists the days "on which the Church requires such a measure of abstinence as is more especially suited to extraordinary acts and exercises of devotion."

The Prayer Book Church Year is a most effective teacher of the Gospel and witness to Jesus Christ. We go with Him through the colorful cyclorama of His life and ministry. Then He goes with us in our lives, our work, our worship, and our recreation. He lives in us when we live in Him. The Holy Communion reminds us of this mutual indwelling. A string of beads illustrates the mutual relationship of the Christian Year and our faith and life. Which is more important, the string or the beads? The answer is that they are both necessary to each other in order to function as a string of beads. The seasons, festivals, and holy days of the Church Year are beads strung on the golden chain of Christ's life. From the Church Year we gain a pattern for the better understanding of our faith and more dedicated Christian living. The Church Year is instructive to Christians and an active witness to all others. It qualifies our faith with its center in Jesus Christ and shows us by precept and example how we are to live as His disciples.

> And now we start it all anew:
> Advent is like . . . some wonderful place
> In the land of beginning again.[2]

QUESTIONS FOR REFLECTION OR DISCUSSION

1. Explain the value of the Prayer Book Church Year to your Baptist neighbor.
2. What are the differences between the Christian Sunday and the Jewish Sabbath?
3. What is the difference between a feast and a fast?
4. Comment on the statement: "The main theme of the Church Year is Jesus Christ."
5. What do B.C. and A.D. mean?
6. Do you notice any similarity between the Prayer Book Church Year and the Christian Creeds?
7. How does the Christian Year testify to Christ?
8. In what ways does the Prayer Book Church Year provide a pattern for Christian living?

[2] Source unknown.

Books for Further Reading

Pell, Walden, and Dawley, Powel M., *The Religion of the Prayer Book*. New York: Morehouse-Barlow Co., 1950.

Perry, Edith, *An Altar Guild Manual*. New York: Morehouse-Barlow Co., Third Ed. 1963.

Wilson, Frank E., *An Outline of the Christian Year*. New York: Morehouse-Barlow Co., 1941.

17

My Part in the Worship of the Church

THE WORSHIP OF THE EPIS-
copal Church, based as it is on the Book of Common Prayer,
is a corporate activity of the Body of Christ. Each parish
church is a fellowship at worship, not merely a group of
individuals worshipping in assembly. The unity of Episcopal
worship is created by a traditionally true motive to worship
inspired by the Holy Spirit and implemented by the Prayer
Book. Archbishop William Temple well describes the high
motivation of the Church's worship: "This only, it seems,
is man's true good—to worship." The corporate worship of
the Church is a regularly provided opportunity for each
Christian to participate in his highest good: divine worship.

The Book of Common Prayer not only provides the
framework and the substance for Christian worship but
also gives directions for the expedient performance thereof.
These directions are called "rubrics" (from Latin *ruber*,
red) because they were once printed in red ink, although
today they are printed in italics or smaller type. Rubrics are
included in the Prayer Book text to make the movements
and actions of worship clear and understandable. They
assist the Church in preserving solemn, impressive, and
beautiful worship accomplished "decently and in order" to
the glory of God and the edification of Christ's Church.

The importance of the individual worshipper and his

part in corporate worship make it necessary for each churchman to consider well his responsibilities within the Church's
worship. Of course, a Christian's worship responsibilities
include frequent prayer, and daily private and family devotions. In these duties an Episcopalian is helped by recourse
to the Prayer Book and other devotional materials. The
Prayer Book will remind him that worship is a primary duty
and then help him to perform it. Regular use of the Prayer
Book will develop good worship habits.

Some special private devotional preparation is almost a
required prerequisite for corporate worship to be personally helpful. Too often the only Sunday morning preparation of a churchman consists of a hurried cup of coffee and
a quick glance at newspaper headlines, sports, or comic section. The man who receives most from the worship of the
Church is the one who reverently prepares his mind and
soul for the rare privilege of taking part in supernatural
communication with God and with the Christian's beloved
Lord and Saviour.

*The sincere churchman will go to his church in plenty of
time (at least ten minutes before the appointed hour) to
continue his preparation for divine worship in his pew.*
On first entering the church, the worshipper will be aware
of the impressive atmosphere the church creates for his inspiration and stimulation. The Episcopal church is always
a place of beauty, from the most simple structure to the
most elaborate and ornate cathedral. Color, architecture—
indeed, all skill and art are combined to call the worshipper
to the purpose of his coming: the adoration of God. Truly,
no setting can be considered too beautiful for the worship
of God in Christ's Church.

The first and central object of the worship of the Church
is Jesus Christ. In the Episcopal church, therefore, an altar

is placed in a central position, to confront each Christian with the symbol of redemption, the cross of Christ, "high and lifted up." The Church usually uses candles on the altar as symbols of the true Light of the world in Jesus Christ, "God of God, Light of Light." Flowers and fair linen also adorn the altar to focus attention on the festive nature of Christian worship as a "feast of the Resurrection."

The Christian enters his church in a reverent and friendly manner. He accepts the assistance of an usher or, in the absence of one, goes quietly to a pew. If a parish bulletin is provided it is given to him by the usher or it will be available in some convenient spot. Many Episcopalians make a reverent bow toward the altar before entering a pew. Such a bow is made also on crossing in front of the altar, at the declaration of belief in Jesus Christ in the Creeds, or when the processional cross passes by. This act of reverence is a sign of respect and humility before Christ. A more extreme act of reverence is the genuflection, in which one knee is touched to the floor. Another act of personal devotion is making the sign of the cross—one of the Church's most ancient customs and the action with which a Christian is signed or sealed in baptism on reception into Christ's flock. Worship in the Episcopal Church permits complete freedom for any individual acts of personal devotion. The important thing is that we show humility and reverence in our worship of God. Just what act or acts of reverence we use is a matter of individual taste or parish custom.

Once in the pew, the worshipper kneels for personal prayer. *In the worship of the Episcopal Church, kneeling is the proper posture for prayer. Episcopalians, therefore, kneel for all prayers except when otherwise directed.* Kneeling expresses the penitence and humility of the Christian before God. It quiets the worshipper and prepares him to hear God speaking. Just what is the content of a worshipper's prayer period before the service begins? As with all private prayer, it will vary from person to person and from time to time. The Prayer Book does provide helps in two large sections, pages 35 to 53 and 587 to 600. Good manuals for such devotions are available for those interested. A personal prayer by each Christian for the rector, the choir, his family, and for every need is always appropriate.

After his preparatory devotions, the churchman waits in quiet anticipation for the service to begin. Continuing in this reverent attitude he never talks loudly in church, keeping silence before God as he is instructed by the Bible. He checks the parish bulletin for hymns, the Collect, Epistle, and Gospel for the day, and for the Psalm. It is always helpful to read over these wonderful parts of the Church's worship. The wise worshipper uses such study to aid his concentration upon holy things and thus train his mind to prevent it from wandering. The interested parishioner studies the bulletin for the parish announcements. He listens with reverent attention to the organ prelude which often is planned to set the tone for the service to come.

When the service begins, the Christian is expected to stand for the processional hymn. Indeed, he is expected to stand for any procession and recession of clergy, choir, and acolytes, who serve as ambassadors of Jesus Christ, the Christian's Lord and King. *Standing is the proper posture for praising God. Episcopalians stand to sing (or say) all hymns, the* Gloria Patri, *the* Gloria in Excelsis, *all canticles, the Psalms, the Gospel, and the Creeds.* It is better to stand before the singing of the hymn begins so that each worshipper may "sing forth" his praise together with the entire congregation. Each member of the congregation is expected to participate in all corporate parts of the service. The full value of worship is best achieved when each worshipper sings or says all responses distinctly and audibly, leaving nothing to others.

Some visitors express surprise that so many parts of the Episcopal service are sung. The hymns, canticles, versicles, and responses are the Christian's opportunity to "sing unto the Lord" as he is bidden. Corporate song can be the most uplifting personal experience in public worship, yet week after week many congregations, assembled to praise as well as pray, stand mute, unmoved to sing. The Hymnal provides tunes and pointings for the *Venite,* the other canticles, and the versicles and responses for all to use. A churchman will profit personally and benefit the parish witness when he joins in to sing with all his heart.

The congregation remains standing until bidden by the minister to kneel for the General Confession in Morning Prayer. In the Holy Communion the worshippers kneel immediately after the processional for the Collect for Purity. A general confession is the opportunity for each Christian to make his confession of sin to Almighty God. A sincere penitent will endeavor to make it an honest confession of personal sins and weaknesses.

Sitting is the proper posture for hearing God's Word and the Church's instruction. Episcopalians sit to listen to the lessons in Morning Prayer, the Epistle in Holy Communion, the announcements, the sermon, and the anthem. Sitting relaxes one more completely. It will assist him to concentrate on the Bible passage or sermon. The one exception to this rule is for the reading of the Gospel in Holy Communion, when the Church asks Christians to stand. Such a gesture is a sign of great love and respect for the words of and about Jesus Christ, our Saviour and Lord.

We stand to sing the canticles after each lesson in Morning Prayer and the *Gloria Tibi* (Glory be to thee) and *Laus Tibi* (Praise be to thee) sung before and after the Gospel in Holy Communion.

All Christians stand to join in the recital of the Creeds. In this corporate recitation, as in the singing or saying of the *Gloria*, it is the general practice of the Church for all people to turn toward the altar. The invitation to pray in the versicles of Morning Prayer calls us to kneel until the Grace (pp. 16, 20). With the reassuring Grace, Morning Prayer is technically over. Modern usage, however, has added announcements, sermon hymn, offertory, presentation sentence, closing prayers, a benediction, and a recessional hymn. The rubrics of the Holy Communion make full provision for announcements, sermon hymn, offertory, and presentation sentence before returning to the Communion service (pp. 71, 73, 74). The importance of the offering in the worship of the Church, and especially in the Holy Communion, is expressed in the presentation sentence "All things come of thee, O Lord, and of thine own have we given thee" (p. 73). The first phrase expresses an open acknowledgment of God's gifts: "creation, preservation, and all the blessings of this life." "Of thine own have we given thee" is a corporate expression of genuine Christian stewardship. It continues the acknowledgment of God's ownership and adds the dedication of our gift to God of self and substance offered with thanksgiving.

Most parishes teach that the call in the Communion service to "pray for the whole state of Christ's Church" is answered by the congregation's kneeling. Many students and followers of the liturgical movement, however, request the worshippers to remain standing until they are bidden to make their "humble confession to Almighty God, devoutly kneeling." As always. the churchman follows the teaching and custom of his own parish. Devout Christians kneel throughout the remainder of the Communion service until they go to the altar rail to receive. In some parishes the ushers guide the communicants in an orderly and reverent procession to the altar. In every case utmost dignity and solemn quiet is to be maintained.

The communicant kneels at the altar rail. He will receive the consecrated bread (wafer) in his hand, usually on the right palm. His right hand is held with the knuckles resting on the palm of the left hand. The bread is lifted directly to the mouth and not taken in the fingers. The wine is received directly from the chalice. The communicant may assist the priest in receiving the chalice by guiding the cup to his lips, taking hold of the base lightly. The one exception is a reception by intinction. In intinction the bread is dipped into the wine and placed directly on the tongue. When intinction is authorized the parish custom is followed. The communicant will wait until the person next but one to him has been communicated before leaving the altar rail. On his return to his pew the worshipper will kneel for his own prayer of thanksgiving. He will remain kneeling, except for the *Gloria in Excelsis,* until the Blessing is given. He will kneel again after the recessional hymn for a moment of silent prayer. In many parishes this final period of personal devotion is accompanied by an extra-liturgical ceremony of the extinguishing of altar candles.

Some concluding observations on other services and a few general advices will be helpful. Evening Prayer is constructed so much like Morning Prayer that the same general responsibilities of the worshipper will apply. The Litany or General Supplication is said or sung kneeling unless in procession, when the congregation stands. It is a service rich with opportunity for the participation of each worshipper. The congregation stands throughout Holy Baptism and the Solemnization of Matrimony, joining reverently in prayers and responses. At a reading of the Burial of the Dead the congregation is expected to participate actively, and usually the Psalms are read responsively.

Some general advices are:

1. Follow the basic churchly rule for worship posture: stand to praise; kneel to pray; sit to listen.

2. Remember normal courtesies in church. Share your Prayer Book and Hymnal with others in the pew and pass the alms basin when indicated.

3. When visiting other parish churches, conform to local customs with reverent attention, following the Prayer Book.

4. When in church for any purpose other than worship, conduct yourself with reverence and dignity, as in God's house. It is customary for women to cover their heads in church.

Some critics of the Episcopal Church disparage the physical motion in the Church's worship. Too much kneeling, rising up, and sitting down, they say! Actually each physical action is designed to produce a spiritual effect. The Church early recognized that outward acts are often a stimulus to inward acts of devotion. Christians therefore continue to offer both body and soul in worship to the glory of God "in spirit and in truth."

Regardless of any outward sign or expression of individual devotion, the churchman who takes an active part in the worship of the Episcopal Church will be aware that in this corporate worship something deep and reverent is expressed. He will appreciate that with "all the company of heaven," the world-wide Christian Church, of which he is a member, and the local parish congregation, with whom he worships, the name of Almighty God is hallowed, the faith of Jesus Christ is confessed, and the inspiration of the Holy Spirit is received. The Christian is now prepared to go forth to contend by his words and deeds for the coming of Christ's Kingdom.

QUESTIONS FOR REFLECTION OR DISCUSSION

1. Explain the difference between the concepts of the Church at worship and individuals worshipping in assembly.
2. How will faithful Prayer Book use develop good worship habits?
3. Why is reverent, personal preparation necessary for effective corporate worship?
4. Answer the criticism: "The Episcopal Church is decorated too elaborately."
5. What reasons can be given for the three traditional worship postures: kneeling, sitting, and standing?
6. What place have individual acts of devotion in the worship of the Church?
7. Does the rule "when in Rome do as the Romans do" apply to personal acts as well as to corporate worship?
8. Is the hiring of professional singers the best means to secure good music in church worship?

BOOKS FOR FURTHER READING

Gifford, Frank D., *The Christian Way.* New York: Morehouse-Barlow Co., 1961.

Smith, H. Robert, *The Church for You.* New York: Seabury Press, 1956.

The Congregation in Church. London: A. R. Mowbray & Co., 1947.

Walker, Charles, *The Ritual Reason Why* (edited by T. I. Ball). London: A. R. Mowbray & Co., 1950.

18

My Quest for Effective Personal Prayer

Pᴇʀꜱᴏɴᴀʟ ᴘʀᴀʏᴇʀ ʜᴀꜱ been called the most neglected resource available to Christians. A majority attend church with some regularity, but few fulfill the recommendation of the Church to pray "in all things." Every adult Christian knows that he ought to pray, that the Christian life is not complete without communion with God. The average Christian, however, is not satisfied with his prayer life. Perhaps it is because he harbors some basic misconceptions regarding prayer. One popular misconception is that Christians pray only for material results. Disciples must learn to pray as the Prodigal Son, who progressed from his demand to "give me" to a petition to "make me" (St. Luke 15:12, 19). With such a primary change of attitude we learn to pray for spiritual results. Another prevalent misconception is that Christians pray only because they think they ought to, following an ill-defined sense of duty. Many adults still use the childhood verse-prayer, "Now I lay me down to sleep . . ." to fulfill their conscience-motivated "duty." However, there can be little reality for an adult in a prayer which is mere childish rote.

Every sincere Christian has available ample instruction and example in private prayer. Jesus Christ is without question the very highest and best example and teacher in the life of prayer. Indeed, prayer was the atmosphere in which our Lord lived. The disciples' early request for help was "Lord, teach us to pray." This request has become the universal cry of all Christians. Notice that Jesus' answer was not "*if* you pray, say . . ." but "*when* you pray, say. . . ." It is obvious that the Master took the prayer life of His followers for granted. Our Lord's very life was prayer. Even on the Cross He used the good-night prayer of Jewish youth taken from the Psalms: "Father, into thy hands I commend my spirit." In this intimacy Jesus revealed Christian prayer to be a living relationship and communion with a personal God and loving Father. In this communication *both* speak and *both* listen. True prayer is always a dialogue and not a monologue. In this harmony of attitude and affection true communion exists. Oddly enough, this true communion was once described by Mohammed. "Angels come . . . both night and day . . . God asketh them how they left his creatures: They say, 'we left them at prayer and we found them at prayer.' "

There are several guides for the Christian to effective personal prayer.

Meaningful prayer must be directed to God and offered to Him with undivided attention. A college student, critical of his Episcopal roommate, said, "He says his prayers in his bed." The object of true Christian prayer is God. So often our prayers go no higher than self because self is the subject with which we are most concerned. What can we do to remedy this situation? A Christian holds God's greatness, goodness, and nearness in his mind and heart and in that way rises above self. Christ taught that God is always available and that He does listen. However, the sincere and prayerful Christian must surrender completely to His will.

Prayer has been called the avenue between self-will and the will of God. To find our way along this avenue we must let the Holy Spirit guide our thoughts and our wills. Only thus will we accomplish the blessed communion of the finite with the Infinite.

Most Christians find it difficult to conquer the problem of wandering thoughts. Unfortunately, the repetition of sing-song prayers learned by rote allows the subconscious mind to wander. What can we do about this? We can concentrate as deeply as possible, centering our minds on God. Some thought, variety, and use of our own words also aids personal prayer. Helpful devotional teachers tell us to conserve our physical and mental energy for prayer and not give God the dregs of the night. Helpful resources are also readily available: for example, the Bible, which is the greatest book of prayer; the Book of Common Prayer, which contains a matchless collection of prayers (if we learn to use it for individual and family prayers, it will become a most vital resource); the Hymnal, which is full of devotional and prayer hymns; other devotional materials such as *Forward Day by Day;* and a personal prayer list of persons and projects.

Rewarding prayer must be well disciplined from without and from within. Outward discipline is important for the growth of rewarding inward personal prayer. Regularity in our prayer life must be carefully planned and the times safeguarded. Of course, we can pray at any time. However, quality is more important than quantity. St. Paul called us to "pray without ceasing" (I Thessalonians 5:17). This may call for the use of ejaculatory prayers, which are merely sentences or thoughts. It would be well for the Christian to plan on setting aside at least ten minutes for prayer every morning and every evening. We must take the necessary time if we wish to develop a successful life of personal prayer. It is also important to arrange a place of prayer. A proper place should be quiet, comfortable, and free from distraction and interruption. In His teaching regarding prayer, Jesus advised a small room and a closed door (St. Matthew 6:6).

Inward discipline is likewise an essential ingredient in an effective life of personal prayer. It is important that we follow a pattern, but with some variety. While framework maintains relevancy without variety, it may sometimes lead to monotony. A pencil and paper for prayer notes often help to clarify thoughts. It is helpful to keep notes on our needs and the needs of others so that they may be presented in an orderly fashion to God in prayer.

It is important to strive to use all of the six essential elements of prayer.

1. The heart of all effective Christian prayer is to *adore* and *praise God*. We reserve only for God, who is worthy of our adoration and praise, our pure exalted gem of personal worship.

2. Christians *confess,* repent, and seek God's forgiveness in prayer. Indeed, Christian prayer would be incomplete without these great elements.

3. Christians *thank God* for everything including "our creation, preservation, and all the blessings of this life" (Book of Common Prayer, p. 19). The General Thanksgiving used in its entirety would be helpful here.

4. *Petition* is a necessary element in personal prayer. Many pray only in petition. Christians think first of God and then of others before asking anything for self. However, the Bible does encourage us to bring our needs and desires before God (Philippians 4:6). Petition is made a worthy

element of prayer by first aligning our wills with God's will.

5. *Intercession* is a Christian's prayer for others. With love we place before God those for whom we implore His healing and salvation. Intercession is essential to strong Christian fellowship. The Church is strengthened as we pray for our family, our friends, and the work of God's Spirit in our parish.

6. *Meditation* and silence are necessary to meaningful personal prayer. A quiet time should be spent by the Christian in which he can listen and wait for God's counsel. With confidence he may "go forth" believing. Or, as Moffatt has translated our Lord's answer to the blind man who was healed, "As you believe, so your prayer is granted" (St. Matthew 9:29).[1]

Effective prayer must be offered as Christ taught His disciples to pray. The "Apostles'" prayer is an eloquent framework and starting place for personal Christian prayer. There are some who say the greatest prayer of all time is the simple petition "Thy will be done . . . (in me)." Our Lord taught His disciples to pray "in faith, believing." According to His teaching there is no unanswered prayer. We may not receive what we ask, but God does give us some answer. Jesus' promise, "My grace is sufficient for thee" (II Corinthians 12:9), is an answer in itself if we can bring ourselves to understand it. Our Lord taught His disciples to pray with perseverance. His parable of the friend and the householder ends with the imperative call to prayer. "Ask, and it shall be given you . . . knock, and it shall be opened" (St. Luke 11:9). The Master's final promise is "that your joy might be full" (St. John 15:11). Our Lord taught His disciples to

[1] James Moffatt, *The Bible: A New Translation* (New York: Harper & Brothers, 1922).

pray in His name. St. John tells us, "Whatsoever ye shall ask the Father in my name, he will give . . ." (16:23). When we have faith in Christ and pray in His name, spirit, and manner, our prayer will be effective.

Prayer has been called the battle line of Christian living. It is not an abstract theory nor a sentimental hope. It is an instrument of the Holy Spirit in Christians. Prayer is a channel from God's fullness to our emptiness, through a living, co-operative relationship. The spiritual force of the ages is available to answer personal Christian necessity on request. A little boy once said to me, "I am praying for you," and immediately I thought of Melancthon's statement, "Brethren, the children are praying for us, take courage!"

It is a Christian's duty, honor, and privilege to open the channel to God through personal prayer. St. Chrysostom wrote, "The monarch vested in his royal robes is far less illustrious than a kneeling Christian ennobled and adorned by communication with his God. What honor was ever conferred like this?" The Duke of Wellington had a habit in old age of answering the clergy's invitation, "Let us pray," with a hoarse whisper, "by all means." Indeed, the Christian must pray "by all means." Is prayer a neglected resource in your life? It need not be. Begin today, using the Lord's Prayer and adding to it according to our Lord's instruction, and you will find the greatest power you have ever known. Alfred, Lord Tennyson, once wrote, "More things are wrought by prayer than this world dreams of." He was right!

QUESTIONS FOR REFLECTION OR DISCUSSION

1. What is your conception of the meaning of prayer?
2. Why must we be taught to pray as were the disciples?

3. How can external preparations be an aid to enter into the spirit of prayer?
4. Name and describe the distinct elements of prayer.
5. Comment on St. Paul's direction to pray "in all things."
6. May we ask God for specific and material things?
7. How would a "rule of life" benefit your resolve to be more faithful in private prayer?
8. Does God always answer our prayers?

Books for Further Reading

Bishop, Shelton H., *The Wonder of Prayer*. New York: Seabury Press, 1959.

Schmuck, Roger C., and Switz, Theodore M., *Growth in Prayer*. New York: Seabury Press (pamphlet).

Wilson, Frank E., *An Outline of Personal Prayer*. New York: Morehouse-Barlow Co., 1937.

19

The Lord's Prayer

THE LORD'S PRAYER COMES to us directly from our Lord, in His own words. Because of its unique origin, it is highly prized and universally used in all Christendom. Indeed, every service in the Book of Common Prayer contains the Lord's Prayer, and, needless to say, every Christian in his private devotions uses this magnificent prayer. Perhaps because the prayer is so familiar and is used so often, it is the victim of over-familiarity which leads only to dull repetition. It is necessary therefore for all Christians to study and know the prayer thoroughly, so that its use can be spiritually refreshing and profitable.

Jesus gave the prayer originally in answer to the universal cry of mankind voiced by His disciples, "Lord, teach us to pray." Jesus' response became one of the priceless treasures of the Christian Church.

It is short enough—only seventy words woven into seven sentences which can be memorized by even the youngest Christian. Its simplicity makes it attractive to all. It is complex enough, however, to contain the comprehensiveness of the entire Christian faith. Some have said it is almost a creed. Regardless of any description or comparison, the Lord's Prayer is truly the prayer of the faithful Christian. The spiritual unity of all of life is vividly illustrated by the "prayer of prayers." It is the prayer for God's Kingdom and will, and yet it is also a prayer for daily bread.

A Christian's understanding of the Lord's Prayer grows as he grows in grace. It has been said, "A child can make it his own, but a saint cannot exhaust its meaning." Henry Ward Beecher once said, "I used to think it a short prayer, but if a man were to be stopped by every word until he had thoroughly prayed it, it would take him a lifetime."

A quick look at this most unique of all prayers will be enlightening. *First of all, it is a prayer to "Our Father."* The use of the plural pronoun is most interesting. No other prayer begins with "Our Father" except those patterned after the Prayer of our Lord. The salutation is startling, commanding, and vital. Because Jesus evidenced such an intimate relationship with His Father, we too have come to have a new dimension in Fatherhood. We call Him "Our Father" because He is the Father of all mankind. The new concept of God as the Father of all, given to us by Jesus Christ, illustrates the family nature of God's Kingdom and of God's created family, mankind. Especially is this true of the family of the Church, whose members are best described as the "Children of God."

We do, of course, worship an Omnipotent, Almighty God. While He is truly our Father, we realize, as the prayer continues, that He is not just "our Father," but "our Father in heaven." Heaven indicates the place of God's glory, the ultimate home of the Christian family and of each individual Christian. Our Lord further points out that God is holy and worthy of being hallowed. The words *holy* and *hallowed* simply mean that God's name is holy and that God alone is worthy to be worshipped by all of His children.

Second, it is a prayer for God's Kingdom. The ideal of the Kingdom of God was most important to Jesus and thus it became important to His Church. The establishment of the Kingdom of God was the principal message of Jesus. It was His first theme and perhaps His only theme. His greatest sermons were preached on the subject of God's Kingdom. His challenge to His disciples, and all those who heard, was, "Seek ye first the kingdom of God, and his righteousness; and all these things shall be added unto you" (St. Matthew 6:33).

Of course, our Lord taught the message of the Kingdom with definite social and missionary implications. It was to be a kingdom built upon outstanding principles and marching under shining banners. It was to rule out all evil, all poverty, and to cause men to understand each other as brothers under one Father, governed by His laws. The Kingdom of God is often described simply as "the rule of God in the hearts of men."

The Lord's Prayer has deep personal, as well as social, implications. A Quaker once suggested that the petition for God's Kingdom could be used with the personal reference, "Thy kingdom come in me." Used in this way, the personal nature of our religion could be more obvious in our lives. The best reading, however, places the emphasis not on "us," nor on "me," but on the word *Thy: "Thy* Kingdom come in me."

Third, it is a prayer for God's will. The coming of God's Kingdom depends upon the sincere application of this petition. One of the saints of the ages has described the spiritual quality, "In His will is my peace." Some have added "victory" to make it read, "In His will is my life and victory."

What is the will of God? It is God's purpose expressed in

Christ. In this petition we come to God and ask Him for a partial understanding of our part in the divine will and work. Only one qualification remains: we must wait for His answer. What we really are asking is, "What wilt thou have me to do?" Jesus Himself used a similar petition in the Garden of Gethsemane, and God answered His prayer with the Cross of Calvary. Again the Quaker's adaptation of the prayer can be used: "Thy will be done in me." Such a petition is most appropriate. The personal equation is obvious in the Lord's Prayer, and when we truly seek God's will, we will surely find God's answer.

Fourth, it is a prayer for daily bread. Christianity does not avoid reference to, and the use of, material things. It is not strange therefore that our Lord included the request for daily bread as a worthy petition in His great prayer. But notice that He puts it in its proper place. He first urges us to acknowledge God, His glory, His goodness, and to acknowledge our creaturely stewardship and our relationship to God, His Kingdom, and His will. Here, however, we are urged to acknowledge God's sustaining power by asking Him to provide for our material needs. In this petition our Lord again uses a plural reference, "Give *us* this day *our* daily bread." It is almost a family prayer. Someone has translated it, "Give us bread needed for the day." You will recognize at once that it is not a petition for luxury, but merely for daily needs—a request for bread, not cake.

Of course, it is not only a petition for material bread, but also for spiritual bread. Jesus Himself teaches us that "Man shall not live by bread alone, but by every word that proceedeth out of the mouth of God" (St. Matthew 4:4). The Holy Communion is an illustration of God's answer to this petition, for in the Sacrament of the Altar we receive not only a symbolic material substance, but also the mystical gift of the "Spiritual Presence of our Lord."

Fifth, it is a prayer for forgiveness as well as for a forgiving spirit. Again, with concern for the whole family of God, we ask forgiveness as we give forgiveness. Of course, the Episcopal Church uses the word *trespasses,* while many other Christians use the word *debts.* Both are correct. Both appear in ancient biblical manuscripts. To argue the case of either word is beside the point. The first emphasis of this petition is the admission of our sins. None can plead "not guilty" before God, for indeed we have all sinned and come short of the glory of God. The wonderful truth implied, however, is that we may be assured that God forgives us. Man's need for forgiveness is universal, as is his need for bread. But we must also learn to forgive! Forgiveness is a necessary quality of a Christian's life. "If ye forgive not men their trespasses, neither will your Father forgive your trespasses" is one of the greatest teachings of our Lord (St. Matthew 6:15). This prayer for forgiveness and the forgiving spirit, therefore, must be part of our striving for the highest qualitative life in Christ.

Sixth, it is a prayer for divine guidance. The puzzling petition which follows often confuses us: "Lead us not into temptation, but deliver us from evil." Does this mean that God tempts us, or that He causes us to be tempted? Indeed, it is not God who tempts us, but Satan. The petition might well read, "Do not allow us to be led into temptation." Since temptation (testing and trial) is common to all men and since it is only with God's aid and guidance that we can overcome it and win the victory, we petition Him for that guidance. Jesus well knew this truth and commanded His Church to teach it. God will give us strength to meet temptation and He will deliver His children from the power of the Evil One.

Finally, the Lord's Prayer concludes with a great doxology to God's glory, or a doxology of God's glory. The doxology appears only in St. Matthew's account of the Lord's Prayer, and not in the one given by St. Luke. The reason for this variance is not known. As a first-century doxology, or early Christian hymn—regardless of why it appears in one place and not the other—it is a universal and ever-glorious expression of Christian hope in God's ultimate victory. "Thine is the kingdom," we say, even though sometimes to voice this assurance seems mere folly. Is our world God's Kingdom? We look about us in terror and wonderment as we behold man's inhumanity to man and his ruthless plundering of the earth's resources. Yet Christians believe He must reign. Indeed, He will!

We ascribe to God "the power and the glory." Well might we ask, "Whose power?" Is it vested in the power of man's "H" bomb, or in the power of man's giant missiles? Not at all. God alone is all-powerful. It is His power and His glory to which men owe their feeble power and life.

The concluding words, "for ever and ever," reveal the magnificence of the doxology. The extra words, "and ever," are used by Episcopalians and others to give the necessary body to the concept of God's continuity and eternity. The same concept is obtained from the meaning of the "Alpha and Omega," the beginning and the ending, and the message of the *Gloria Patri:* "As it [the Holy Trinity] was in the beginning, is now, and ever shall be, world without end. Amen." Thus the stirring doxology enables the Prayer of our Lord to end on a note of joyous and triumphant praise.

The Lord's Prayer is rightly called the world's greatest prayer. It is rivaled only by the "high-priestly prayer" used by our Lord in the Upper Room as part of a very select instruction of the Apostles privileged to hear His last discourses (St. John 17). But the Lord's Prayer was given for all Christians. It is an extension of Christ's teaching and example, intended by the Master to be the keystone of our prayers.

The world's greatest prayer is at once a bulwark to Christian faith and a redeeming vessel of Christian unity. Using the prayer given by the Christian's common Lord and Master, it is possible for those of all communions to worship together. Some may use the word *debts,* while others use the word *trespasses.* Some may stop at the ending of the Lucan version, and some may not use the final "and ever." But all Christians are one in the use of the Lord's Prayer.

There is a story which reveals that at the sinking of the ocean liner S.S. *Titanic* someone said, "Shouldn't we say a prayer together?" As if in unison response, they began the Lord's Prayer—Roman Catholics, Methodists, Presbyterians, others—each perhaps with a word or two different, but each praying to a common God, well knowing that this prayer of our Lord was the prayer of life, both in time and for eternity.

QUESTIONS FOR REFLECTION OR DISCUSSION

1. What does the statement "The Lord's Prayer is truly the prayer of the faithful Christian" mean to you?
2. Defend the use of the plural pronoun *our* so often in the prayer.
3. How can God be both "almighty Creator" and "our Father"?

4. Explain to a pagan why a Christian is willing to pray for and accept God's Kingdom and God's will as binding entities in his life.

5. Discuss the relationship of the Fatherhood of God and the brotherhood of man.

6. Answer the charge that the petition for daily bread is not worthy of the rest of the prayer because it is "too material."

7. Comment on man's dual need to be forgiven and to forgive.

8. How does God act toward us in temptation and evil?

BOOKS FOR FURTHER READING

Green, Bryan, *Being and Believing*. New York: Charles Scribner's Sons, 1956.

Martin, Hugh, *The Lord's Prayer*. London: Student Christian Movement Press, 1951.

Simcox, Carroll E., *Living the Lord's Prayer*. New York: Morehouse-Barlow Co., 1951.

Underhill, Evelyn, *Fruits of the Spirit, Light of Christ, and Abba: Mediations on the Lord's Prayer*. New York: David McKay Co., 1956.

20

The Christian and the Ten Commandments

THE TEN COMMANDMENTS are contemporary and relevant to the modern Christian. As God's revealed law, they are basic to all human law and necessary to the intelligent interrelations of all mankind. The Decalogue, which is Greek for "ten words," should be used often in the Church, so that its significance can be recalled more easily. The Ten Commandments are God's law, traditionally believed to have been written on tablets of stone and received on Mount Sinai by the great Jewish patriarch, Moses. The Ten Commandments are the unrepudiated "law" of Christianity. Christ said that He did not come to destroy the law, but to fulfill it in Himself. Further, He gave a masterful summary of the law to underline its universal and timeless quality.

According to St. Paul, the law was but the God-given schoolmaster which was to bring men to Christ. For a Christian, the keeping of the law is no easy job, as it was no easy job for the Jew, nor is it an easy way to heaven. The Decalogue is a series of signposts displaying necessary directions for living the Christian life. The Ten Commandments are more than just a series of laws or statutes. They are God's law, the moral law —part of life's reality, molded from human experience. To a certain degree, you "catch yourself" in relation to the Decalogue, since there is a natural consciousness of right and wrong written in the hearts of men. The law simply spotlights our failures more starkly. A short poem from the pen of James Russell Lowell very well illustrates the ingrown nature of the Decalogue.

> In vain we call old notions fudge,
> And bend our conscience to our dealing;
> The Ten Commandments will not budge,
> And stealing will continue stealing.[1]

A summary look at each unit of the Decalogue will bear rewarding compensations. The Ten Commandments begin with four theological laws, laws implying faith in God and outlining our duty to Him. Then follow six social and moral laws, underlining our relationship toward others and our responsibility to them.

The First Commandment, "I am the Lord thy God; Thou shalt have none other gods but me," challenges us with the primacy and the absoluteness of God. There is "none other" than He. While this was intended to speak to the idolatry of the past, it also speaks to the idolatry of the present, our modern indifference and our practical atheism. We moderns are materialists, with material things as gods. The First Commandment calls us to task with a recital of the fact that there is but one true God, and nothing, or no one, is to be set above Him. Christian attitudes of belief and worship make mandatory our fealty and obedience to Him.

The Second Commandment insists, "Thou shalt not make to thyself any graven image . . . thou shalt not bow down to them, nor worship them." In spite of God's commandment,

---

[1] *Motto of the American Copyright League* (November 20, 1885).

we make a variety of idols for our worship. The first two commandments insist that nothing should distract our souls from the worship of God. Worship comes from "worthship." Thus true worship can come only from the adoration and reverence of God, the "all mighty" and the "all worthy." Indeed, only that which is of God and that which He inspires is worthy of our worship.

The Third Commandment insists, "Thou shalt not take the Name of the Lord thy God in vain." Indeed, Jesus taught us to pray, "hallowed be thy Name." Christians should protest the profaning of God's name. The name of God and His Son express God's character and goodness. Of course, it is not profane when we name God's name with a holy reverence in our hearts, and/or with a sense of "worthship." When we use God's name, our usage should remind us of the high character and innate goodness of His very presence in our lives.

The Fourth Commandment insists, "Remember that thou keep holy the Sabbath-day." This reminder speaks to our stewardship toward God—our duty on the Sabbath day. It therefore calls all Christians to a proper apportionment of their time to praise and glorify God. Since all that we are is God's, even our time and its use, it is our duty to see that we use our time for God's glory and for His Kingdom. Our "bounden duty" is to set aside one day to worship God and a fair proportion of our lives to serve Him. The Book of Common Prayer calls us to "worship God every Sunday in his Church; and to work and pray and give for the spread of his kingdom" (p. 291).

The Fifth Commandment insists, "Honour thy father and thy mother." The word *honor* as used here means love, respect, and reverence. We are told that charity begins at home and this adage, of course, is true. It is also true in the Christian sense, for the first sphere of the Christian's responsibility is to his loved ones. Dr. Charles Mayo once said, "The wisest thing we [the Mayo brothers] ever did was to choose our parents." Unfortunately, responsibility for parents is something that many moderns too often forget. The Jewish people are far ahead of the Christians here, for they have built upon the faith of the Ten Commandments a fundamental respect for elders and for the authority of the family.

The Sixth Commandment bluntly insists, "Thou shalt do no murder." God alone must decide the termination of the life He has created. Murder is never justified. The defense of country, home, and loved ones, however, and perhaps the edicts of the civil authority, are considered as exceptions. There is also spiritual murder. Our Lord Himself taught that the man who hates his brother is already a murderer. It is important, therefore, for us not only to renounce the committing of physical murder, but also spiritual murder, caused by bitter hatred of another.

The Seventh Commandment, "Thou shalt not commit adultery," is an important divine prohibition. Adultery means a "mixing up," which is the best description of the word available. The outside person mixes up God's state of marriage, which in a real sense is a crime not alone against man, but against God as well. Since Christians are under the jurisdiction of God's law, obedience to this commandment is necessary to preserve Christian marriage and thus preserve personal faith and morality. Regardless of our modern sophistication, chastity is God's way; His moral law still stands.

The Eighth Commandment insists, "Thou shalt not steal." Again we confront an ancient and time-tested law of God and man. The right to own private property is guaranteed in both the natural and the statute law. Of course, many evil practices all about us are very close to the borderline of stealing. Many of these practices are thought excusable. Those who were in the service remember it was commonly held that to steal from the United States Government was excusable. This was rationalized by the idea that "we pay taxes, don't we?" Further, to millions of Americans, dishonesty on income tax forms is standard practice. The time for tightening our moral standards and elevating personal morality is overdue. The Book of Common Prayer urges us "to be true and just in all our dealings," and "to keep our hands from picking and stealing" (p. 580).

The Ninth Commandment, "Thou shalt not bear false witness against thy neighbour," is a very broad prohibition. It regulates all human relations where the tongue is concerned. Of course, there are only a few who would take an oath on the Bible and then commit false witness or perjury. There are many, however, who commit false witness daily with "little" lies and petty gossip. False witness is a blow at personal honor and public justice, and is a sin not alone against our brother man, but also against God.

The Tenth Commandment insists, "Thou shalt not covet." Men covet things without knowing that covetousness is involved. A neighbor's mode of life and all the things that he has which we desire for our own, come within the realm of covetousness. The Tenth Commandment, far ahead of its time, anticipates the teaching in Proverbs 23:7, "As [a man] thinketh in his heart, so is he," and our Lord's teaching which suggests that a man's thoughts are the picture of his character (see St. Matthew 5:28).

An example of covetousness is seen in the visit of a small child to the five-and-dime store. He sees a toy; he wants the toy. Told he cannot have it, he begins to cry and sulk, and becomes quite nasty. But it is not only children who are guilty of such covetousness. Each of us has it in our hearts to break this law.

In summary we recall that the first four commandments are theological in nature. They have to do with God and our duty to Him. We are commanded to worship only Him, to keep from idolatry, to hallow His name, and to keep holy His day. The last six are social and moral in character. The Fifth Commandment urges us to begin our charity and responsibility at home, and the next three command that under God's law and under the common laws of society, we shall not murder, commit adultery, nor steal. The final two commandments also give us a common law from God and man—we shall not bear false witness and we shall not be covetous.

Our Lord's magnificent summary of the law is a superb positive statement of the true nature of a Christian's life. Jesus said, "Thou shalt love the Lord thy God with all thy heart, and with all thy soul, and with all thy mind. This is the first and great commandment. And the second is like unto it, Thou shalt love thy neighbour as thyself." Indeed, Jesus then added as if in emphasis, "On these two commandments hang all the law and the prophets" (St. Matthew 22:37-40). Christians are to be content with nothing less than the keeping of the "summary" to love God and our neighbors since it is our Lord's explicit command.

The Book of Common Prayer in "A Catechism" (pp. 579-580) offers matchless teaching regarding a Christian's duty toward God and his neighbor.

My duty towards God is To believe in him, to fear him, And to love him with all my heart, with all my mind, with all my soul, and with all my strength: To worship him, to give him thanks: To put my whole trust in him, to call upon him: To honour his holy Name and his Word: And to serve him truly all the days of my life. . . . My duty towards my Neighbour is To love him as myself, and to do to all men as I would they should do unto me: To love, honour, and succour my father and mother: To honour and obey the civil authority. . . . To hurt nobody by word or deed: To be true and just in all my dealings: To bear no malice nor hatred in my heart: To keep my hands from picking and stealing, and my tongue from evil speaking, lying, and slandering: To keep my body in temperance, soberness, and chastity: Not to covet nor desire other men's goods; But to learn and labour truly to get mine own living, And to do my duty in that state of life unto which it shall please God to call me.

The keeping of the commandments is an almost impossible task, but we are not dismissed from the responsibility of trying. We must pray more faithfully for God's special grace to learn to obey His will and commandments and to serve Him. With divine help we will begin loving and stop hating; we will begin serving and put aside personal selfishness. When we accept God's will as our own, and when we apply Christ's summary of the law to our lives, we will then begin truly to live as Christians.

Questions for Reflection or Discussion

1. How do you account for the universal nature and character of the Ten Commandments?
2. Answer the charge that the negative tone of the Decalogue is "repelling."

3. Prepare a list of the same commandments phrased in a positive tone throughout.
4. Comment on the statement: "The Ten Commandments should be brought up to date and rewritten to suit modern conditions."
5. Explain what Jesus Christ meant by His teaching that He came not to destroy the law, but to fulfill it.
6. Describe to your Jewish neighbor the implications of the similarity of Jesus' summary of the law to the Decalogue.
7. Discuss the statement that since it is impossible to keep the commandments, they may be disregarded.
8. What is the relationship between the Decalogue, the moral law, and the common law?

BOOKS FOR FURTHER READING

Green, Bryan, *Being and Believing*. New York: Charles Scribner's Sons, 1956.

Herklots, H. G. G., *The Ten Commandments and Modern Man*. New York: Oxford University Press (Essential Books), 1958.

Simcox, Carroll E., *Living the Ten Commandments*. New York: Morehouse-Barlow Co., 1952.

21

The Bible and the Church

OUR AGE HAS BEEN LA-
beled with some justification an age of indifference to the
Holy Scriptures. While the Bible itself is truly the textbook
of the Church and indeed a best seller on every bookstore
list, it often impresses us as a highly irrelevant book. A frequent joke among clergymen is that many people dust off the
Bible just before the visit of their pastor rather than have him
see its unused condition. The Episcopal Church calls upon its
young people and adults to join in a modern movement to
restore the Bible to widespread contemporary use.

There are two roadblocks in our modern thinking regarding the Bible. The word *Holy* seems to set it apart and make it
different from any other book. Actually the word merely in-
fers the presence of the Holy Spirit in the writing and preservation of the Scriptures. Another roadblock is the claim on
the part of some sects to the infallibility of the Bible. The
extreme claim that the Holy Scriptures are the dictated
"words" of God rather than the revealed Word of God often
drives people away from, rather than to, the use of the Bible.

The Episcopal Church recommends intelligent and patient
individual, family, and group study and use of the Holy Scriptures. The Church's teaching program has urged group and

individual investigation into the background and meaning of the Scriptures in history and the application of the Bible in our modern life. It is said that one of the chief contributions of Anglicanism to modern Christendom has been the widespread dissemination of the English Bible and the encouragement of individual Christians to use and read it.

Some questions and answers concerning the Holy Scriptures follow.

1. *What is the Bible?* The Greek words *ta biblia* mean the books or library. The Bible is truly a library of books, with the marks of the human authors on every page. The works of many different authors, with different characters and moods, are presented in its pages. These many men used widely different styles and literary forms throughout. The Bible is a library of religious literature culled from the actual religious experience of many men. As indicated above, the infallibility of the Bible is an idolatry to be denied. Some Protestant sects claim to "exalt" the Bible. Episcopalians do not "exalt" anything or anyone but the Christ. The Bible was not dictated in heaven and carried to earth by angels. The Holy Scriptures are a record of human souls in contact with God and were written by men in their own way. Jesus used the Scriptures to teach everyday living as from a book dealing with day-by-day life.

2. *Is the Bible the Word of God?* Again denying idolatry, we must immediately affirm that in the Bible God spoke to the world through His chosen authors. Note, however, it was God speaking *to men through men*. It was the author who recorded God's message and expressed it in the best way possible, at that time. This action is known as divine revelation. Of course the highest revelation—*the Word*—is Jesus Christ.

He is the theme and measurement of the Bible. All before Him points toward Him and He is the New Testament. As St. John so aptly said, "The Word was made flesh, and dwelt among us, and we beheld his glory" (St. John 1:14).

3. *Is the Bible the work of God the Holy Spirit?* The Church teaches that the influence of the Holy Spirit accounted for the writing and preservation of the Holy Scriptures, but always through men who were under His direct and holy inspiration. Again, it was not dictation; it was influence and inspiration. In the Bible, God is the chief actor moving within all of the scenes. He through His Son and the Holy Spirit is the unity of the Holy Scriptures—its inspiration.

4. *How did we get our Bible?* Centuries of inspiration, progress, and development went into the writing and preservation of the Holy Scriptures. The earliest writings of the Old Testament, beginning about 1,000 B.C., were in the ancient Hebrew script, which contained no vowels. As pure Hebrew ceased to be spoken, marginal notes of vowels and accents (the *Masora*) preserved the meaning of the text, but it was not until sometime between the fifth and eighth centuries A.D. that this Masoretic text was formally written out. Meanwhile, during the last few centuries before the birth of Christ, versions of the Hebrew Scriptures had also become available in Aramaic, the popular family tongue of the Semitic people, and in Greek, the international language of the day.

We have often heard of the "canons of the Scriptures." The word *canon* in this connection means the collection of books accepted as genuine and inspired Holy Scriptures. The canon of the Old Testament was finally settled by the Council of Jamnia in A.D. 90. It was limited to the books that were understood to have been written before the time of Ezra the Prophet.

The New Testament canon is an entirely different subject. The unique development of the New Testament is so marked because it was the literature of a movement beginning in Christ and then moving through the Apostles and into His Church. The Epistles (letters) of St. Paul and others writing to the early churches came first. St. Paul's manuscripts are dated from about A.D. 50 and onward. The first Gospel, the Gospel according to St. Mark, was not written until about A.D. 70. From these writings the Church gained the expression and witness of the experience of the early Christians. In these manuscripts from widely scattered areas we read the full biographies of their leaders and the counsels and advices of the Apostles writing to the far-flung missionary parishes.

The canon of the New Testament was settled at the Third Council of Carthage in A.D. 397. How did the Council work? Can we trust its judgment? What were the principles used for choosing the books to be included? The first criterion the Council set was, "Is it a book of Apostolic origin?" The second, "Is the book part of the Christian heritage and spirit?" The third, "Is the book used in the public worship of the Church?" As you can see, the Church was constantly the author and preserver of its textbook. Commenting on the relationship of the Church and the Bible someone has said, "The Church is to teach and the Bible is to prove." The Episcopal Church in describing the use of the Bible has said: "All Scriptures are given by God and are profitable for doctrine." Every clergyman ordained must agree that he will support his faith upon the evidence of the Holy Scriptures.

5. *What are the major divisions of the Holy Scriptures? The Old Testament,* of course, contains the pre-Christian sacred

literature of the Jews. It teaches religious truth through history available from no other source; law which still influences modern law; poetry which contains some of the glorious songs that we sing in the canticles; and prophecy which points us to Christ and calls our attention to a more adequate social life influenced by religion. The Old Testament seemed binding on Christ and on the Apostolic Church. In many places in the New Testament the "fulfillment of the Scriptures" is seen to be Christ Himself. St. Paul's writings are full of references to the Old Testament. The Old Testament is important for us today because it is the background of the New Testament.

The *Apocrypha* is a group of fourteen books which were excluded from the Old Testament canon when it was settled in A.D. 90. Written probably between 300 B.C. and A.D. 70, the books had found their way into the Greek version of the Old Testament and so were received by the early Church. They are still included as part of the Old Testament in Roman Catholic editions of the Bible, but in many Protestant editions they are omitted entirely; when they appear at all, it is as a separate section between the Old and New Testaments. The Episcopal Church uses lessons from the Apocrypha in Morning and Evening Prayer. The Apocrypha is valuable because of the picture it gives of historical developments between the end of the Old Testament and the beginning of the Christian era. It records the story of the search for human redemption, which is accomplished in the Gospel of Jesus Christ.

In the *New Testament* we learn how God the Son completed the work of revelation and redemption which is the good news of the New Testament. We also find the record of the Church, the Body of Christ, living and witnessing to the truth of His life, His resurrection, and His promise of eternal life.

6. *Is there any unity in the Bible?* The unity of the Bible is achieved through God. A single organic theme runs through the entire Bible: God in action in history to assure man's redemption. The Person of Jesus Christ—the Word—upholds the revelation and truth of the Bible. The Church was produced through the Holy Spirit's mission and guidance to reveal and to teach the truth. Obviously the Bible early became necessary to give testimony to God's mighty acts and prove the teaching of the Church. It is a book of life, teaching us the relationship of a living God to a living people.

It is necessary for all Christians to assume that corporate and individual use of the Bible is important to the Church and also to the life and witness of every disciple. Some people will say that they find it difficult to read the Bible. With these people most would agree. However, if a Christian will take up his reading with prayer and with a genuine intention to hear God's Word he will find instruction and guidance for daily living. For help in this regard we should eavesdrop on the interesting conversation between Prudence and Matthew in *Pilgrim's Progress.* Prudence, the catechizer, asks Matthew, "What do you think of the Bible?" He answers, "It is the holy word of God." Prudence says, "Is there nothing written therein but what you can understand?" Matthew answers, "Yes, a great deal." Prudence says, "What do you do when you meet with such places . . . ?" Matthew's answer is classic: "I think God is wiser than I. I pray that he will please to let me know all there is that he knows will be for me good." If we would approach the Bible with this humble, yet determined, attitude, we would gain much profit and good for ourselves and our families. The Bible is the Church's book. Guided by the Holy Spirit and taught by the Church, we will be strengthened and nourished in our faith by the wise and patient use of the Holy Bible.

QUESTIONS FOR REFLECTION OR DISCUSSION

1. What do the words *Holy* and *Bible* mean?
2. Does the Church teach that God wrote the Bible or that He inspired its writing? Explain the answer.
3. If God *inspired* the writing of the Bible, is every word therefore *infallible?*
4. How is the Old Testament of value to Christians?
5. Answer: "The Church was founded upon the Bible."
6. Answer: "We can't believe the Bible because most of it was 'made up' at Church Councils."
7. Explain to a pagan how we got our Bible and defend its authenticity.
8. How many reasons can you give for reading the Bible?

BOOKS FOR FURTHER READING

Chase, Mary Ellen, *The Bible and the Common Reader*. New York: The Macmillan Company, rev. ed. 1952.

Dentan, Robert C., *The Holy Scriptures*. New York: Seabury Press, 1949.

Goodspeed, Edgar J., *The Story of the Bible*. Chicago: University of Chicago Press, 1936.

Grant, Frederic, *How to Read the Bible*. New York: Morehouse-Barlow Co., 1956.

Wilson, Frank E., *An Outline of the New Testament*. New York: Morehouse-Barlow Co., 1935.

Wilson, Frank E., *An Outline of the Old Testament and Apocrypha*. New York: Morehouse-Barlow Co., 1935.

22

The Healing Ministry
of the Church

THE POST-RESURRECTION
Upper Room appearance of Jesus to the Apostles, described
by St. Mark, presents a most interesting and challenging lesson to the modern Church. After He had severely upbraided
their minimum faith, our Lord commanded them to go forth
to preach and baptize. He promised that a special sign of their
ministry would be outstanding success in divine healing.
"They shall lay hands on the sick, and they shall recover" (St.
Mark 16:18). Healing was without question a vital part of
Christ's ministry. His teaching on the subject and examples
of divine healings performed by Him can be found in thirty-
seven separate New Testament accounts.[1] The number of
those healed probably would total in the thousands. This is
a most conservative estimate from sources limited by the gos-
pellers' preoccupation and overwhelming interest in the saving grace of Christ. The evangelists' presumption was that
salvation applied to all of life. The modern lesson here is in
the better understanding of the word *salvation*. The Latin
word *salus*, meaning health or wholeness, is closely related.

The forms of healing used by Jesus were quite varied. In
one case our Lord placed clay on the eyes of a blind man and

[1] See *The Ministry of Healing*, by John Ellis Large (New York:
Morehouse-Barlow Co., 1959) , Chapter XIII.

urged him to go and wash the clay off to be completely healed. In other cases Jesus laid His hands on the sick, the dying, and the dead to accomplish healing. Always His form of healing was accompanied by a spoken word of faith. The New Testament record reveals that Jesus considered no form of sickness incurable. Indeed, our Lord raised a man who had been pronounced dead. The only condition He ever asked of those to be healed was faith and repentance, two factors equally important in healing. Modern medicine is returning to the truth that the whole person is to be healed, not only the body but the soul or spirit (psyche). The Church can offer much counsel on this truth.

Following the example and teaching of Jesus Christ, the Apostolic ministry of healing plays a very prominent role in the record of the growth and influence of the Church. There are ten distinct accounts of healing through the Apostles in the New Testament.[2] One of the most striking is the story of how St. Peter and St. John healed the cripple on their way to the Temple (Acts 3:6-7). It is gripping mainly because the man asked not for healing but for alms. Peter offered the only treasure that he could, the power of Christ to heal through the laying on of Apostolic hands. St. James describes the common healing ministry and experience of the Church more vividly than any other New Testament author. He counsels, "Is any among you afflicted? let him pray. . . . Is any sick among you? let him call for the elders of the church; and let them pray over him, anointing him with oil in the name of the Lord: and the prayer of faith shall save the sick, and the Lord shall raise him up" (5:13-15).

*The Church has always "at all times and in all places"
believed and taught that Christ does heal through His dis-*
[2] *Ibid.*

ciples. The Church, beginning with the Apostles and continuing down to about the ninth century, took the healing ministry of Christ for granted. The first-century churches were called "temples of healing," and every illness of the members of this new community was presented to Christ for healing through the Church. Medieval disuse by the Western Church of the healing rite diminished and restricted its application until it became, in the hands of the Roman Catholic Church, a sacrament of the dying. Its very title, Extreme Unction, is a clue to its character in the Roman Catholic Church. Of all the Western Churches, the Anglican Church alone held to and made vital the original characteristics of the healing ministry of the Church. The Protestant Episcopal Church restored a brief form of unction in the 1928 revision of the Book of Common Prayer.

The Church still has a vital healing ministry through Jesus Christ. Our Lord still offers the only answer to human suffering which is reasonable and helpful. Pain, suffering, and death are inescapable and inevitable human factors for which many substitute religions and philosophies have tried to offer an answer—but they all fail at this point. There are those who would deny the existence of pain, suffering, and death: e.g., the Christian Science advocates who create what is called a spiritual diversion, hoping the material reality will go away. There are those who, like the stoics of old, call for the individual to have a "stiff upper lip" and bear pain, suffering, and death with dignity. The Christian Church, however, at the foot of Christ's Cross knows and shares the answer to pain, suffering, and death. Through its Divine Sufferer the Cross brings divine grace to strengthen those who would seek God's healing power. Indeed, the Prayer Book includes prayers which voice individual repentance and confidence in God's forgiving and restoring power, and also petitions for personal fortitude, patience, and the restoration of individual health as God wills.

The Church acknowledges the partnership of medical science and persons of other related arts in the healing ministry. Christians will appreciate with interest the relationship and similarity through the Latin word *cura* of the words *care* and *cure*. As we have noted above, the Church has always taught that true healing must be concerned with the whole man, his body as well as his soul or spirit. Therefore, the Church has always urged co-operation of all partners—physician, nurse, clergy, and family. To underline this a Christian physician has counseled, "In the light of what we now know, if I, as a whole person, am not treating a whole person, I might as well be practicing veterinary medicine." There is no substitute in the interpersonal ministry of healing for the care and skill of the physician and other members of the medical team, who, along with the Church and family, are ministers and partners with God in the healing process.

A new general attitude regarding healing is most promising. Dr. A. J. Cantor, President Emeritus of the Academy of Psychosomatic Medicine, has been reported as saying, "Perhaps the time is coming when pills and prayers will be prescribed together." An English doctor has written in a British medical journal, "There is not one tissue in the human body wholly removed from the influence of the spirit [psyche]." The Church is no stranger to this truth. Indeed, Christians know there is no part of the human body beyond God's healing power and love. A clergyman shared with me an interesting case involving two hospitalized members of his parish. The two parishioners had the same illness and were in the same stage of recovery. However, one was in great distress and pain, and the other comfortable and relaxed. While this is hard to understand on the surface, the role of the mind and spirit (psyche) explains the difference. A four-month survey of the Massachusetts General Hospital Out-Patient Clinic (conducted by Doctors Stockle, Davidson, and Weinberger) disclosed that 80 per cent of the patients seen had no organic illness related to the symptoms they reported and that 84 per cent of the patients seen had psychiatric problems.

Christians may take heart at the news that on every hand a modern revival of spiritual ministration in the illness of church members is growing. The Episcopal Church is taking the lead in spiritual healing, advocating the use of unction administered by the clergy. Holy Unction in the Prayer Book includes a prayer plus the laying on of hands or the anointing with oil with an appropriate blessing in the name of the Lord Jesus Christ. The thousands of reports from this ministry coming from such groups as the Order of St. Luke are almost as amazing as are the New Testament accounts. One miracle accomplished recently concerned the Reverend Canon Clifton Best of the Diocese of Harrisburg, a priest who has been mightily used by Christ in a healing ministry. A woman who had been stricken for years with multiple sclerosis was healed by Christ through this believing, devoted servant, by instruction, prayer, and the laying on of hands.

Will unction always heal? This is an interesting question and deserves an answer. Unction, when combined with medicine and faith, always helps. The healing is accomplished by Christ. Believing that our Lord urges us to continue to bring our physical needs to Him in faith, how can we fail to find help from the services provided by His Church?

The Prayer Book does provide the means for bringing Christ's power to heal into our lives. We need not only to understand its benefits but also to be aware of its limitations. The Church teaches no magic. It teaches that healing is a reasonable combination of God-given intelligence in the form of the medical minister, the faith of the patient and his family, and the healing ministration of the Church. Each member of the Church is urged to pray for the sick. Each Christian is asked to pray for his minister that this man may be a vessel of Christ's healing power. By all means a Christian should never hesitate to call upon the Church for the ministry of healing in faith, believing. The story of Jesus healing the blind man in His home town should encourage us. He said to the blind man, "Do you believe that I can do this?" When the man answered "yes," our Lord healed and assured him, saying, "Have what your faith expects"[3] (St. Matthew 9:29). Moffatt translates this startling statement, "As you believe, so your prayer is granted."[4] Do you believe that Christ can still heal? The Church answers "yes" for us. Christ's Church continues His healing ministry to augment that of modern medicine. With the physician the Church is a partner in the care and the cure, the wholeness and the health of those who come in penitence. in prayer, and with faith believing.

> Faith came singing into my room
> And other guests took flight,
> Grief and anxiety, fear and gloom
> Sped out into the night.
>
> I wondered that such peace could be,
> But faith said gently, "Don't you see
> That they can never live with me?"
> —Anonymous[5]

[3] J. M. Powis Smith and Edgar J. Goodspeed, *The Complete Bible, An American Translation* (Chicago: University of Chicago Press, 1939).

[4] James Moffatt, *The Bible: A New Translation* (New York: Harper & Brothers, 1922).

[5] Quoted from *Sharing, A Journal of Christian Healing.*

QUESTIONS FOR REFLECTION OR DISCUSSION

1. Does the New Testament support the claim that healing was a vital part of Jesus Christ's ministry?
2. Comment on the statement: "Jesus considered no form of sickness incurable."
3. Were the disciples commissioned to heal in Christ's name as well as to preach and baptize?
4. Why were early Christian churches called "temples of healing"?
5. Compare the Episcopal Church's Office of Unction with Roman Catholic Extreme Unction.
6. What other partners does the Church acknowledge in the ministry of healing?
7. How does Christ still heal?
8. Will spiritual ministration in illness always heal?

BOOKS FOR FURTHER READIN'

Gross, Don, *The Case for Spiritual Healing*. New York: Thomas Nelson & Sons, 1958.

Large, John Ellis, *The Ministry of Healing*. New York: Morehouse-Barlow Co., 1959.

Neal, Emily Gardiner, *A Reporter Finds God Through Spiritual Healing*. New York: Morehouse-Barlow Co., 1956.

Sharing, A Journal of Christian Healing. San Diego, Calif.: St. Luke's Press (periodical).

Spread, R. A. R., *Stretching Forth Thine Hand to Heal*. London: Skeffington & Son, Ltd., 1936.

23

The World Mission of the Church

THIS CHAPTER WILL BE NO apology for missions, for one is never in order. Every Christian, however, needs to be reminded of the magnificent mission of the Church of Christ whenever and wherever it has been and continues to be at work in the world. The misconception common to many shallow people is that the Christian mission is the special work carried on elsewhere by a few eccentric people with a peculiar vocation. Some unthinking Christians accept P. T. Forsythe's tongue-in-cheek definition, "Missions . . . [are] a kind of hobby carried on by the Church instead of belonging to the very being and fidelity of the Church." The Christian mission is neither a luxury nor a "necessary evil" in the life and work of the Church. It is absolutely an integral part of the Christian faith. Such mission is related to, and an extension of, the very Gospel of Christ, the "good news" of God's mighty acts in Christ for man's salvation. It is the missionary implication of the proclamation (kerygma) itself, and is identified with, and the by-product of, the Christian faith. The Christian believes in one God the Creator and Preserver of all men, the bond of human brotherhood and the source of divine love. He also believes in one Lord Jesus Christ, Saviour and Redeemer, Incarnate God on a mission of divine redemption. It is Christ Himself who becomes, with the believer's acceptance, his motive for

Christian mission. The Christian also believes in the Holy Ghost, the holiness and strengthener of the Church, the divine inspiration of the redemptive community, and the guide of the Christian mission in the world.

The Christian mission is a dynamic movement stemming from the very power and Person of Jesus Christ. The potential of Christianity has always been and remains tremendous. The early Church proved the staggering success of the mission of the Church of Christ against seemingly overwhelming odds. Today the Church is highly organized and boasts the most favorable statistics. It has weekly "propaganda" meetings. It has means at its disposal for mass communication through press, radio, and TV to enlarge the already great potential. What the American Communists could do with the organization and set-up of the Christian Church! Indeed, Christians may never reckon Communism out of the picture anywhere, for world Communism is a missionary-minded movement, hopeful of winning the whole world for its political and social philosophy. By comparison modern Christianity lacks the Holy Spirit-inspired passion for the conversion of the world that was dominant in the early Church. Since the Church is the only agency possessing the "good news" today, it must proclaim it. With St. Paul our watchword must become "Woe is . . . me, if I preach not the gospel!" (I Corinthians 9:16). Only a working, witnessing Church will fulfill the high missionary imperative given to us directly by our Lord.

A study of some of the truths about the Christian mission might be helpful.

The Christian mission is Christ Himself. He was sent on a mission from God. The New Testament has several references to this original mission: "God sent forth his Son" (Galatians

4:4); and again, "God sent not his Son . . . to condemn the world; but that the world through him might be saved" (St. John 3:17). Jesus is quoted by the author of the Epistle to the Hebrews as saying, "Lo, I come to do thy will" (10:7). Our Lord was the first missionary. Jesus' consecrated, dauntless missionary spirit should be a helpful example to all His followers. He spoke of His mission often, adding, "that the scriptures might be fulfilled." The titles Christ took reveal His missionary spirit: "Son of Man," which comes from the Old Testament Prophet Daniel; "Servant of God," which has its source in Isaiah; and "King," which is a title for the Messiah given by the Psalmist. To His disciples the Blessed Lord declared with climactic authority, "I and my Father are one" (St. John 10:30).

Jesus Christ's ministry was a missionary ministry. Over and over again He described His mission as "seeking and saving the lost." Our Lord's missionary journeys took Him from Nazareth to Galilee, across the Jordan to Perea, through Samaria, to minister to His own in Judea, and finally to die outside of Jerusalem. The Cross of Calvary is the symbol and the meaning of Christ's mission. From St. John's magnificent Evangel we read the words, "God so loved the world, that he gave his only begotten son" (3:16). This manifestation of divine love was accomplished by Christ's action on the Cross. He was "obedient unto death, even the death of the cross" (Philippians 2:8). This holy mission of the Man of Calvary is continued in His disciples, in individuals, and in a special group known as the Christian Church.

Christ called His Apostles to share in His mission. The very definition of the word *apostle* has a missionary connotation. An apostle was a witness to the Resurrection. A missionary Himself, our Lord made missionaries of His Apostles, who were called "that he might send them forth" (St. Mark 3:14). Jesus did send them forth, two by two, to preach repentance, heal the sick, and proclaim the Kingdom of God. He also used a somewhat larger group of disciples commissioned as missionaries. The Master sent this group forth two by two in advance of His coming to prepare for His coming into the several cities He visited. His Apostles, however, were ordained and commissioned for mission in a special way. Jesus told them, "As my Father hath sent me, even so send I you . . . ye shall be witnesses . . . unto the uttermost part of the earth" (St. John 20:21; Acts 1:8).

Obeying Christ's direct command, the Church made Christian mission its primary method. The concluding statement of St. Mark's Gospel gives a strong clue to the missionary method of the early Church: "And they went forth, and preached every where, the Lord working with them, and confirming the word with signs following. Amen" (16:20). The Acts of the Apostles and all the Epistles confirm the presence and success of this vital Christian mission. St. Peter, St. John, and St. Paul write of Spirit-filled preaching, of the baptism of hundreds into the Church, of Spirit-guided healing, teaching, and swelling of the Church in every land.

The illustrious successors to the twelve Apostles have put together a most impressive missionary record. The history of the world knows no other organization with such vital and dynamic growth. A modern missionary, Mackay of Uganda, testified in his *Journal* to the Gospel-motivated truth which is the secret of the Church's success, "Am I not the link between dying men and the dying Christ?" The Christian mission is the continuing story of the development of the Church. Early church history is full of the accounts of missionary labors. The Church spread to Asia Minor, to Europe, and to Africa through the tremendous labors of St. Paul and his immediate group. The second century saw the Church established all around the Mediterranean and as far north as Great Britain. Christian missionary labors won Europe, crossed the Atlantic to win America, and reached as far as Africa and the Orient. Motivated by Christ and led by the power of the Holy Spirit, missionaries aimed to win the world for the Christian Church.

The missionary function of the modern Church became almost a purely institutional activity. The Roman Catholic Church and some Protestant groups have been more prolific in the field of institutional missionary activity than the Episcopal Church. However, wherever Christian missionaries have gone forth there has been some cohesion of "fellowship." Frankly, there also has been some embarrassment caused when denominational missionary societies overlapped and were contradictory in spirit and teaching. In general the Church's mission has always shared a common goal and method. True to Christ's charge, the Church has sent missionaries to the uttermost parts of the earth. These devoted disciples have often had to cope with overwhelming hardships, yet they would agree with David Livingstone, who humbly said, "I have never made a sacrifice."

True to Christ's example, the mission-established Church has been nurtured and native leaders have been trained. Indigenous churches with native clergy are the key to modern Christian missions. The Bible and the Prayer Book have been translated into many native tongues to aid the young churches. Indeed, the Church's influence in certain lands has been far in excess of the statistics of membership. For example, the Hindu reforms in India were greatly influenced by the Christian missions there. Also the work of the Episcopal Church in Liberia is outstanding. Liberia has been a self-governing state since 1847, aided by church educational and agricultural missions.

True to Christ's teachings, the Christian mission has always been performed at a personal level. Interested in every aspect of human life—education, healing, and services—the Church has well demonstrated practical Christianity. The Reverend J. D. Theertha, an Indian clergyman, has written, "Hereafter India will be in no mood to receive foreign saviours or foreign masters . . . she wants sons and daughters of Christ who will live in India thoroughly Christian lives, [and] demonstrate by precept and example what Christianity means to them."[1]

The world mission of the Church is still part of the primitive missionary imperative. Make no mistake, we are still within the era of the primitive Church. This is no abstraction; it is a hard concrete fact. Christianity grew as a Church led by missionary laity. Since the laity are the "people of God's mission," the need of the modern Church is not more organization, but personal missionary zeal, work, and prayer. The need of the modern Church is not to fill the churches, but to bring people to Christ. The need of the modern Church is not campaigns for any reason whatsoever, but a Spirit-filled Church led by militant missionary-witnesses. The need of the modern Church is to demonstrate an interest in every person everywhere that he might come to hear the Gospel and know Christ's redemption. The need of the modern Church is to train and equip Christian laymen to be able (like their Communist counterparts) to give a reason for the hope that is in them (I Peter 3:15). A Chinese Communist is reported to have said to a Christian, "Just where do you think

[1] Max Warren, *The Christian Mission* (London: Student Christian Movement Press, 1951), p. 109.

your Christianity will get you?" The Christian countered, "How far do you think your materialism will get you?"

The world mission of the Church will be consummated. This is the Christian's hope and victory. St. Paul said, "He hath put all things under his feet" (I Corinthians 15:27). The Christian mission is the opportunity for all Christians to help bring in the Kingdom of God and put all things under Christ's feet. Enlisted in Christ's mission at baptism as "soldiers and servants," we have a responsibility to "work and pray and give" for the spread of Christ's Kingdom (Book of Common Prayer, p. 291). The Church Militant must be mobilized for the winning of the world for Christ. The Church calls each Christian to do his duty in the world mission led by Jesus Christ Himself.

Questions for Reflection or Discussion

1. How are the Christian mission and Christian missions related?
2. Answer the charge that Christian mission is a special work carried on elsewhere by missionary specialists.
3. Is the Christian mission an integral part of the Christian Gospel?
4. How can the Christian layman be trained to match his Communist counterpart?
5. It has been said that the day of the overseas mission society is past. What is your opinion?
6. Do you consider medical-educational services as part of the Christian mission?
7. How can a growing native church be called the success of the Christian mission?
8. In what ways do you believe you are responsible for the Christian mission?

Books for Further Reading

Addison, James T., *The Episcopal Church in the United States.* New York: Charles Scribner's Sons, 1951.

Dawley, Powel M., *Chapters in Church History.* New York: Seabury Press, 1950.

Manross, William W., *A History of the American Episcopal Church.* New York: Morehouse-Barlow Co., rev. ed. 1959.

Warren, Max, *Challenge and Response.* New York: Morehouse-Barlow Co., 1959.

24

The Anglican Communion

THE DEFINITION OF THE word *Anglican* in the Glossary of this book will provide a helpful jumping-off place for a discussion of the Anglican Communion. "Anglican" there is defined as *"pertaining to the Church of England or to one of a closely related world-wide family of national Churches in communion (fellowship) with it."* A meeting of all the bishops of the Anglican Communion at the Lambeth Conference in 1930 defined this communion as "a Fellowship within the One, Holy, Catholic, and Apostolic Church, of those duly constituted dioceses, provinces or regional Churches in communion with the See [the diocese and bishops] of Canterbury."

Both definitions are precise. The word *communion* itself means a body of Christians having one common faith and discipline, and sharing an intimate and mutual intercourse in a community of interrelation and participation. The Anglican Communion, therefore, is both a fellowship of those churches with one historical focus and a family of many autonomous churches, but without the usual sectarian implication.

Anglicans have a common historical focus in the Church of England. She is our Mother Church. We have, through her, a common heritage, an historical, ecclesiastical genealogy in the

New Testament, in the Apostolic Church, a heritage rooted in Antioch and developed under the leadership of all the outstanding Christians from Augustine to Cranmer. Yet while Mother Church is our link with our Apostolic heritage, still she willingly accepts the maturity and independence of her offspring.

The Anglican Communion is a unique sort of fellowship. We are a family of eighteen autonomous national churches and a number of missionary dioceses united with and through a great parity of faith through the Creeds, of worship through the Book of Common Prayer, of government through bishops, of ministry, evangelism, and life.

Two statements, made by the Archbishop of Canterbury and the Presiding Bishop of the Episcopal Church in 1954, underline our unique nature. The Archbishop of Canterbury said that we are "many different people and races who share in the great tradition, scriptural, Catholic and Reformed, of the Anglican Communion . . . and in the work entrusted to our fellowship by our Lord and Saviour Jesus Christ."[1] Bishop Sherrill said, "We are not regimented through force, but are bound together by ties greater because they are so largely invisible . . . a tremendous center of unity in our common faith and worship, in our heritage, and in our hope for the future."[2]

The structure of the Anglican Communion is a paradox of centralized and yet de-centralized authority and adhesiveness. There is no Anglican pope to assure centralization. There is, however, a basic unit. The Lambeth Conference of 1930 upheld the ancient Catholic principle that the fundamental unit of church organization is the diocese. under the

[1] *Pan Anglican*, Epiphany, 1954, p. 11.
[2] *Ibid.*, p. 9.

jurisdiction of the bishop. Historically the over-all authority in the early Church was held to be the Council (and counsel) of diocesan bishops. The ancient Catholic authority—bishops meeting in council—continued through many centuries until the separation between East and West ended the Councils.

The English Church took up the Council principle and developed it to its modern high point in the Lambeth Conferences, which were begun in the mid-nineteenth century and developed throughout the modern period under such great archbishops as Randall Davidson, Frederick Temple, William Temple, and Geoffrey Fisher. Anglican bishops meet together only to discuss common concerns. They attempt no legislation and demand no adherence to their decisions except that which is implicit in loyalty alone.

A quick look at the various units of the Anglican Communion serves to illustrate its world-wide nature. Statistically speaking, Anglicanism is a free and voluntary association of some 340 dioceses including well over forty million baptized members. (The latest figures give a total of 40,479,472 members, but to this should be added the membership of sixteen dioceses for which no current figures are available.) It is extremely difficult to obtain accurate and up-to-date statistics from all the far-flung parishes of the Anglican Communion. The figures that follow are of necessity only approximate, but they are in each case the most recent figures currently available as listed in four source books.[3]

[3] *The Episcopal Church Annual 1961* (New York: Morehouse-Barlow Co.).

The Official Year-Book of the Church of England 1961 (London: The Church Information Office of the Church Assembly).

Crockford's Clerical Directory 1959-60 (London: Oxford University Press).

John Seville Higgins, *One Faith and Fellowship* (Greenwich: Seabury Press, 1958).

1. *The Church of England*, with 43 dioceses in its two provinces, has 27,005,000 members.
2. *The Church in Wales*, with 6 dioceses, has 750,000 members.
3. *The Church of Ireland*, with 14 dioceses in its two provinces, has 480,000 members.
4. *The Episcopal Church in Scotland*, with 7 dioceses, has 107,344 members.
5. *The Anglican Church of Canada*, with 28 dioceses in its four provinces, has 1,590,897 members.
6. *The Church in the Province of the West Indies*, with 8 dioceses, has 896,890 members.
7. *The Church of India, Pakistan, Burma, and Ceylon*, with 16 dioceses, has at least 457,879 members.
8. *The Jurisdiction of the Archbishop in Jerusalem*, with 5 dioceses, has at least 56,000 members.
9. *The Nippon Seikokai (Holy Catholic Church in Japan)*, with 10 dioceses, has 42,410 members.
10. *The Chung Hua Sheng Kung Hui (Holy Catholic Church in China)*, with 14 dioceses, had 42,000 members when information was last received. In addition, there are 20,000 members in the detached diocese of Victoria, Hong Kong.
11. *The Church of the Province of Central Africa*, with 4 dioceses, has at least 100,000 members.
12. *The Church of the Province of South Africa*, with 14 dioceses, has 929,927 members.
13. *The Church of the Province of West Africa*, with 10 dioceses, has at least 338,621 members.
14. *The Church of the Province of East Africa*, with 5 dioceses, has at least 127,570 members.
15. *The Church of the Province of Uganda and Ruanda-Urundi* (formed in 1961), with 8 dioceses, has at least 420,960 members.

16. *The Church of England in Australia and Tasmania,* with 22 dioceses in its four provinces and 3 extra-provincial dioceses, has at least 2,986,009 members.

17. *The Church of the Province of New Zealand,* with 9 dioceses, has at least 564,000 members.

18. *Dioceses holding Mission from the See of Canterbury* are found in South America, Bermuda, Korea, Borneo, Singapore and Malaya, Madagascar, Mauritius, Gibraltar, and North Africa. These 9 dioceses have at least 119,700 members.

19. *The Protestant Episcopal Church in the United States of America,* with 87 dioceses and missionary districts in its eight provinces, has 3,175,424 members. In addition, it has 61,139 members in 6 extra-continental missionary districts and 207,702 members in 11 overseas missions.

The unique characteristics of the Anglican Communion were most eloquently spelled out by Geoffrey Francis Fisher, then Archbishop of Canterbury, in a great address to the General Convention in 1946 under the heading of the three major elements of Anglicanism.

The first he labeled the Catholic element. This element includes the continuity, tradition, and life of the Church, the very Body of Christ, as the appointed channel of divine grace through the Creeds, the ministry, and the Sacraments.

The second he called the Reformed element. This element emphasizes the Gospel, the Holy Scriptures, as equated with tradition; the evangelical fervor as equated with the Sacraments; and the immediate activity of the Holy Spirit as equated with a certain historic continuity of the Church itself.

The archbishop then pointed to the third element which he called a uniquely Anglican element in Christendom. This element holds an inclusive harmony of both Catholic and

Reformed tradition and lives in a mutual enrichment based upon both. Its characteristics are moderation of judgment, moral earnestness, integrity of purpose, and Christian understanding. He concluded his great address by saying:

> I would say that it is the real strength and glory and special responsibility of the Anglican Churches that they hold together these three elements in our fellowship without resort either to schism or suppression. For all these elements are essential parts of the Christian Faith already visible in the New Testament; they need each other. . . . The truth of Christ should hold them together in Him.[4]

The Anglican Communion in herself is a model of church unity. She has always been vitally interested in Christian reunion. The story of the Philippine Independent Church is an illustration of this interest. One hundred Philippine Roman Catholic priests along with hundreds of thousands of laymen seceded from the Roman Catholic Church and asked for a bestowal of Apostolic Succession from the Anglican Communion. The Protestant Episcopal Church brought it about not only without a required merger pact or concordat of faith, but with only the request that the Philippine Independent Church accept the Apostolic Quadrilateral of Lambeth, decided in 1888, as a declaration on reunion or a standard for intercommunion. The four basic fundamentals are as pertinent now as they were when issued.

1. The Holy Scriptures . . . as being the rule and ultimate standard of faith.
2. The Apostles' and Nicene Creeds . . . as the sufficient standard of faith.
3. The two Sacraments ordained by Christ Himself.
4. The historic Episcopate.

[4] Quoted from *The Living Church,* September 22, 1946.

While the Philippine bestowal was a very successful venture in the field of reunion, other such ventures have been recorded. Full communion has been established by the Anglican Communion with the Old Catholic Church of Europe, the Polish National Catholic Church of the United States; and partial intercommunion with the Church of Sweden.

Anglicans may also be proud of a long and virile record of leadership in the Ecumenical Movement. The word *Ecumenical* means the world-wide Christian community, or the Church as a whole. Bishop Charles Brent of the United States, Archbishop William Temple, and Archbishop Geoffrey Fisher have been leaders in this Ecumenical Movement.

The World Council of Churches had as its early presidents both Archbishop Fisher and Presiding Bishop Henry K. Sherrill. Other leaders in the great World Council of Churches have been Bishop G. K. A. Bell of the Church of England and Canon Theodore Wedel, President of the House of Deputies of the Episcopal Church.

The National Council of the Churches of Christ in the United States of America, as well as the many national councils throughout the world, has had Anglican leadership at all levels.

While it is an established policy for Anglican Churches to strive toward Christian unity, the Lambeth Encyclical of 1948 says ". . . meanwhile it is our duty to make the life and witness of our own Communion strong and effective for its own work." This declaration has produced four major tasks or emphases of the Anglican Communion.

1. A "Cycle of Prayer" for use within the Anglican Communion. In this moving intercessory program we find a spiritual bond of prayer to hold us together.
2. A central college for post-ordination study and scholarship, which meets at St. Augustine's, Canterbury.

3. An advisory council on missionary strategy which will seek to advance co-operation among Anglicans in the Church's world mission.

4. An Anglican Congress in which bishops and delegates from every diocese meet. It has been described as a sort of "spiritual parliament," although it is only a consultative body to the whole Church.

A most appropriate conclusion is contained in the closing remarks of the Archbishop of Canterbury's address at the 1946 General Convention:

> If I have spoken only of this communion to which we belong, it is partly because it is natural for one who holds my office with its historic place in that communion so to do; it is partly because to that communion I owe all I am and give all the loyalty of my heart; it is yet more because I believe that as God has done great things, for all our faults, for us and through us, so God still has a work for us to do, of great moment for Him, for His redeeming purpose, for the whole Church and for the world.[5]

QUESTIONS FOR REFLECTION OR DISCUSSION

1. Comment on the suggestion that another title for the Anglican Communion should be found because of the nationalist reference of the word *Anglican*.

2. Compare the relationship of the Episcopal Church to the Archbishop of Canterbury with that of the Roman Church to the Pope.

3. Substantiate the claim that the Lambeth Conferences are the Anglican counterpart of the Apostolic Councils.

4. Contrast the role of the Lambeth Conference with that of the Anglican Congress.

[5] *Ibid.*

5. How is the tension of the Catholic and Reformed elements of Anglicanism its "real strength and glory and special responsibility"?
6. Describe the establishment of intercommunion with the Philippine Independent Church.
7. Explain to your sectarian neighbor the Lambeth Quadrilateral declaration on intercommunion and reunion.
8. Locate on a map of the world the autonomous national Churches and missionary dioceses of the Anglican Communion.

BOOKS FOR FURTHER READING

Ellison, Gerald, *The Anglican Communion, Past and Future.* New York: Seabury Press, 1960.

More, Paul E., and Cross, F. L., *Anglicanism.* New York: Seabury Press, 1957.

Morgan, Dewi, *Agenda for Anglicans.* New York: Morehouse-Barlow Co., 1963.

Rawlinson, A. E. J., *The Anglican Communion in Christendom.* London: Society for Promoting Christian Knowledge, 1960.

The Anglican Congress, 1963. New York: Seabury Press, 1963.

The Episcopal Church Annual (List of the Anglican Episcopate). New York: Morehouse-Barlow Co.

The Lambeth Conference Report 1958. New York: Seabury Press, 1958.

25

The Church's Unity
in Christ

ALL CHRISTENDOM IS CON-
cerned with reunion. The problem of Christian unity is no
longer the province of a few wishful-thinking idealists. Under
the shocking influence of two World Wars, continuing tension
in the international scene, the challenge of a common enemy
in the form of atheistic materialism, Christians have come to
the point of asking each other, "Must we be forever divided?"
Contemporary hard-thinking concern for reunion has re-
placed the sentimental, sanguine approach which was so
prevalent for a great many years. Longing and simple good
will are not enough to answer the many problems of Christian
reunion. The road toward reunion is a hard one and needs a
great spiritual energy and above all unconditional consecration on the part of all to the cause of Jesus Christ.

Aware of our grievous divisions, our mutual prayer is, as in
Apostolic days, "Come, Holy Spirit, move us, bless us, en-
lighten us, heal us." Confronted with the pastoral prayer of
our Lord with His disciples in the Upper Room as He prepared to accept the Cross for *us*, our consciences are disturbed
with the burden and sin of our present division. Our corporate
sin is that the world does not see us as "one Body in (and of)
Christ," and therefore we lack unity in our witness to the
pagan world. It was written of the early Church, "See how

these Christians love one another." Many pagans in our day could well write, "See how little these Christians love one another." However, there are good signs along the road.

The external witness of the Body of Christ is aided by our mutually desired effort toward understanding one another. The ecumenical or international Christian conferences reveal the great importance of fellowship between the confessional groups. The brotherly atmosphere present is an aid toward reunion. Within our heightened understanding we have come to accept the fact and principle that while the spirit of comprehensiveness is good, the basic differences between us cannot be minimized. We all agree that Christian doctrine and discipline must be preserved. The insistence of the leaders of ecumenical meetings on the study and discussion of Christology, the meaning of Jesus Christ to our day, is most heartening.

Our increasing fellowship leads us to an awareness of the fact that prayer together is needed. Interprayer seems the most logical place to begin. This is the first step in the realm of intercommunion so often suggested by Dr. Geoffrey Fisher, while he was Archbishop of Canterbury. He urged interprayer and study toward unity among all Christians, with intercession for the work and the action of the Holy Spirit in Christ's Church and in our hearts. Five churches in the small Pennsylvania town of Honesdale are in the vanguard of this movement. Baptist, Methodist, Presbyterian, Episcopal, and Lutheran congregations invite their neighbors to worship with them on alternate Sunday evenings. All five clergymen assist in the service with one pastor assigned as the preacher. This is unity at work.

Another interesting sign is the general admission that there are obstacles to corporate reunion. Difficulties involving human tensions and emotion will not be overcome overnight. Age-old historical divisions firmly established through natural, legal, social, and cultural patterns keep us apart. Someone has written tellingly, "It took fifteen centuries to divide the Church, how can we reunite it within fifty years?"

There is also the area of tension between the Catholic and Protestant traditions. One extreme is individualistic Protestantism. The other is the Church of Rome. Karl Barth is quoted as saying, "The only attitude toward Catholics is to try to convert them, not to unite with them." Conversely, Powel M. Dawley has written, "It is useless to pretend that the movement for Church unity can achieve more than a partial approximation to the will of the Lord without . . . the Roman Church."[1] This is an extremely volatile situation, and one which must be handled with great care. It exists, however, and must be considered as a real obstacle to corporate reunion.

There are, however, some positive aspects to some of the so-called obstacles in the road to unity. Geoffrey Fisher, as Archbishop of Canterbury, called to our attention the positive advantage inherent in the sharper definition of denominational tenets and the increased awareness of them by the faithful. Dr. Fisher said that as these definitions are developed, as loyalties are strengthened, as strong doctrine is intensified in every communion, there is a greater chance of reunion. In an illustration the archbishop said, "It is easier to have reunion with a skeleton than with a jelly-fish."

All Christians praying for reunion must acknowledge, with St. Paul, that Jesus Christ is the only foundation for such unity. Our real meeting place is in Christ the Incarnate God. Modern ecumenical meetings have issued strong statements

[1] *Chapters in Church History* (Greenwich: Seabury Press, 1950), pp. 253-254.

concerning Jesus Christ, the Son of God. The difficulty remains in the interpretations made by groups colored with extreme individualism. Any discussion with members of other communions about the Incarnation of the Son of God reveals all sorts of opinions regarding His presence in the world of men as very God. Unity studies must insist on and secure the acceptance of Jesus Christ as God and Saviour by each participant. This is the center of the Church's teaching. The Church's life starts with Christ, points to Him, and will end with His victory. Here is the crisis of modern Christendom.

There is a minimum prerequisite for reunion. It is faith in the Son of God; faith that He is our Church, that His light is our way, that His Body is our salvation. Armed with such faith, the Church will mirror the *ecclesia* (the "called forth") of the New Testament, by new and redeeming fellowship in Him. All doctrine rests upon this fundamental dogma. Belief in Christ, the Incarnate God, is the very foundation and rock of all Christian faith and order. In this dogma we find the Trinity supported. In it we find the only explanation of the divine redemption of mankind. The Incarnation heralds the great acts of God in the world for the salvation of man through Jesus Christ. Here we find the meaning of the judgment of man and his hope through Christ of eternal life. Faith in the Church as the continuation of the work of salvation begun in Christ Jesus is the reason for the Christian missionary imperative.

It is often taught among us that a group of Christians came first and the Church followed. This is not true. Christ came. He is the Church, and into the Church He draws disciples and into the Church the disciples draw other Christians. This is a different frame of reference. Here is institutional and also personal life defined within the unity of Christ's Church. In this light personal life in Him and continuity in His Church are one. Through personal faith in Christ, discipleship, and fellowship with Him in His Church we maintain our continuity, our oneness. Historic ecumenical teaching identifies the work and authority of the Church with the work and authority of our Lord. The Anglican concept of unity transmitted through the Church and the historic Episcopate is a respected contribution at this point.

The most penetrating contribution of the movement toward Christian unity is the growing meaningfulness of the liturgy, the Holy Communion. It is meaningful to all Christians because the Lord's Supper is regarded as the meeting place of Jesus Christ and the faithful. The sacramental life of the Church is not an issue for negotiation. The thanksgiving of Christians for the benefits of the sacrifice of our Lord, poured out in prayers and in communion with the Christ, is not a matter of debate, nor indeed a matter of ordinance. Professor George Florovsky, the great scholar of the Russian Orthodox Church, addressing the Assembly of the World Council of Churches, made this statement which sums up the essence of Eucharistic doctrine: "The Church of Christ is one in the Eucharist, for the Eucharist is Christ Himself, and He sacramentally abides in the Church, which is His Body." The Anglican Book of Common Prayer contributes greatly to progress in the liturgical movement and is a standard for Christian worship among many communions today.

Aided by the foregoing signs on the road, the one Body in Christ witnesses its unity to our pagan world. Underlying our witness is the conviction that unity in one faith, faith in Jesus Christ as God Incarnate, is the first goal of reunion. Whoever believes on the divine Son of God is in the vanguard of reunion. Unity is in Him, and in His Body, the Church, which is and ever will be one. Many misinterpret that great hymn, "The Church's one foundation" (No. 396, The Hymnal 1940). Here is meant *the* Church, not the churches. It might even read, "The Church has one foundation, in Jesus Christ, her Lord." The Church is one in Him. It is not divided, it is one and ever will be one.

St. Paul, in his first letter to the Church in Corinth, calls our attention to that great truth that we are members not in an individual or local community of believers. We are members together in Jesus Christ, and we are members one of another. Christians who live in Him will love and seek after unity within the Body of Christ. Those who are in Him will work to fulfill His petition in His great pastoral prayer, when He prayed that the Church "may be one in us" (St. John 17:21). Notice the qualification: in *us*. St. John shows that the Church is forever united in God the Father and God the Son.

In Jesus Christ we may achieve unity *now;* as a German theologian has described it, *Einheit ohne Vereinigung* (unity without union), unity of love, true to the command of our Lord, "A new commandment I give unto you, That ye love one another" (St. John 13:34). But hear His final identifying commission: "By this shall all men know that ye are my disciples" (St. John 13:35). Unity in His love is the witness of the Christian Church to the pagan world. The Church is one Body in Jesus Christ.

QUESTIONS FOR REFLECTION OR DISCUSSION

1. Explain why the "Lambeth Quadrilateral" on approaches to reunion sets the following minimum standard for Christian reunion:

(1) The Bible as the rule and ultimate standard of faith.

(2) The Apostles' and Nicene Creeds.

(3) The two Sacraments ordained by Christ Himself—Baptism and the Supper of the Lord.

(4) The historic Episcopate.

2. What is the extent of our freedom as Episcopalians, with regard to the above statements, etc.?

3. Why does the Episcopal Church attach so much importance to the Creeds?

4. Why is the Episcopal Church concerned at all with the Ecumenical Movement?

5. How does the Episcopal Church stand today in relation to (1) Rome, and (2) Protestantism?

6. Why has the Episcopal Church been called the *via media*? Is this good?

7. Comment on the statement: "In Christ we may achieve true unity now."

8. How is the Anglican Communion a good model for Christian reunion movements?

Books for Further Reading

Bell, G. K. A., *Christian Unity: The Anglican Position.* London: Hodder and Stoughton, 1948.

Moss, C. B., *What Do We Mean by Reunion?* London: Society for Promoting Christian Knowledge, 1953.

A Short Glossary
of Key Words for Episcopalians

ABSOLUTION—God's forgiveness (and release from sin) expressed by a priest or a bishop following confession.

ABSTINENCE—A reduction in quality of meals (usually by omitting meat) or the giving up of other pleasures, in fasting or self-discipline. See *Fast*.

ACADEMIC HOOD—A hood denoting a scholastic degree, worn over the surplice from the shoulders down the back.

ACOLYTE—One who assists in the worship of the Church as a crucifer, a server, or in some other role.

ALB—A full-length linen garment worn with Eucharistic vestments.

ALTAR—The Holy Table in the church, where the Holy Communion is celebrated and offerings are presented.

AMEN—A prayer response meaning "verily" or "so be it."

AMICE—A linen neckpiece worn with the alb.

ANGLICAN—Pertaining to the Church of England or to one of a closely related world-wide family of national Churches in communion (fellowship) with it.

ANTE-COMMUNION—The service of the Holy Communion through the Creed, or through the sermon if there is one. (See Book of Common Prayer, pp. 67-73.)

APOCRYPHA—The "other" (or "hidden") books of the Bible, not included in the Old or New Testaments.

APOSTLE—One who is "sent forth," a messenger of Christ's resurrection. Usually refers to one of the original twelve disciples and their successors. "Apostolic" means of or relating to the Apostles.

ARCHDEACON—A priest who is given authority by the bishop over a prescribed missionary work within a diocese.

ASCENSION—The miraculous return of Jesus Christ to heaven after His resurrection.

ATONEMENT—The divine act by which God restored the broken relationship between Himself and man through Jesus Christ.

BAPTISTRY—The place in the church, often near an entrance, where the baptismal font is located.

BISHOP—The chief pastor and administrator, the "overseer" of a diocese.

ARCHBISHOP—A bishop who presides over a Province (several dioceses). This title is used in England, Canada, etc., but not in the United States.

BISHOP COADJUTOR—A bishop elected to assist and eventually to succeed the bishop of a diocese.

SUFFRAGAN BISHOP—A bishop elected only to assist the bishop of a diocese, without the right of succession.

MISSIONARY BISHOP—A bishop elected by the General Convention or the House of Bishops to be "overseer" of a missionary district.

BURSE—A square case used to hold the corporal and purificators, etc., and placed on the veiled chalice.

CANON—(1) A law of the Church. (2) A minister who serves on the staff of a cathedral. (3) A "rule" or standard authorized by the Church, e.g., the canon of Scripture—the authorized books of the Bible.

CANTICLE—A short song taken from the Bible and used in Morning or Evening Prayer.

CASSOCK—A long basic garment worn by the clergy, choristers, and acolytes.

CATECHUMEN—One who is being prepared (taught the catechism) for confirmation.

CATHEDRAL—The church where the bishop has his chair and pastorate.

CATHOLIC—A word which means universal, of all. (See Book of Common Prayer, p. 291.)

CELIBACY—The state of remaining unmarried (required of Roman Catholic clergy and religious orders).

CHALICE—The cup used for the wine in the Holy Communion.

CHASUBLE—The outer Eucharistic vestment.

CHIMERE—A long sleeveless garment worn by a bishop.

CHRISTOLOGY—A study of the doctrines relating to Jesus Christ.

CIBORIUM—A chalice-like cup with a cover used to hold the bread for the Holy Communion.

CINCTURE—A belt girding the cassock or alb.

COLLECT—A prayer written for public use which "collects" or sums up the prayers of all.

COMMUNICANT—One who is baptized and confirmed and a member in good standing of his parish church.

CONFESSION—A corporate or individual acknowledgment of sin to God in humility and penitence.

CONFIRMATION—A rite conferred by a bishop which gives the more mature Christians the continued grace and strengthening of the Holy Spirit.

CONSCIENCE—The ability to distinguish right from wrong and the inward guidance of a Christian by the Holy Spirit to choose the right.

CONVERSION—A change of heart, mind, and life by a personal acceptance of Jesus Christ.

COPE—A long cloak sometimes worn by the clergy in procession.

CORPORAL—A square linen cloth upon which the Communion vessels are placed.

CORPORATE—Socially united with a single purpose, e.g., the Church as one in worship.

COTTA—A short white garment worn by choristers and acolytes over a cassock.

COVENANT—An agreement binding upon two parties, e.g., Moses' covenant with God.

CRÈCHE—A manger scene depicting the Nativity of Jesus Christ.

CREDENCE—A shelf upon which the elements are placed in readiness for the Holy Communion.

CREED—A statement of faith held and believed by the Christian Church.

CROZIER—The bishop's pastoral staff symbolizing a shepherd's crook and carried by or before a bishop in procession.

CRUCIFER—The acolyte who carries the cross in procession.

CURATE—A minister elected to assist a priest in a parish church.

DEACON—A minister who has received the first ordination and must serve a probationary period under a priest or a bishop.

DEAN—(1) The presiding minister of a cathedral. (2) The head of a theological seminary. (3) The chief administrator of a college or university.

DECALOGUE—The Ten Commandments. (Greek for ten words.)

DOCTRINE—A technical religious teaching or instruction.

DOGMA—A religious truth revealed by God and defined by the authority of the Church.

ECUMENICAL—A word referring to the world-wide Christian community, the Church.

EMBER DAYS—Days on which the Prayer Book urges prayer for those about to be ordained. They occur four times a year: in Advent, Lent, Pentecost, and September.

EPISCOPAL—Pertaining to or governed by bishops. (From the Greek *episkopos*.)

EPISTLE—(1) A letter, commonly a New Testament letter written by an Apostle. (2) The first of the two passages of Scripture read in the celebration of the Holy Communion, usually taken from one of the New Testament Epistles.

EUCHARIST—The celebration of the Holy Communion as a service and offering of thanksgiving.

EVANGELICAL—Pertaining to reformed Christianity and designating reformed emphasis on the "good news" of the saving grace of Christ. (Derived from the Greek word for "gospel.")

FAST—A day (or a season) on which some self-discipline is recommended by the Prayer Book, usually observed by reduction in quantity of food or drink. See *Abstinence*.

FEAST—A day (or a season) on which holy rejoicing is recommended by the Prayer Book.

FERIA—A weekday, especially one that is neither a feast nor a fast.

FERIAL USE—A musical observance of worship in a plain and simple mode.

FESTAL USE—A musical observance of worship in a joyful and more elaborate mode.

FORGIVENESS—Giving up resentment or claim of offense and granting pardon. A uniquely Christian teaching based on God's forgiveness assured in Christ.

GODPARENTS (SPONSORS)—Persons who represent a child in Holy Baptism by accepting the vows in his name and undertaking the responsibility to share in his Christian environment.

GOSPEL—(1) The "good news" of God's mighty work in and through Jesus Christ for the salvation of man. (2) One of the four Gospels in the Bible, which present the record of the life and teaching of Jesus. (3) The second of the two passages of Scripture read in the celebration of the Holy Communion, taken from one of the four Gospels.

GRACE—The God-given gift of the saving power of Christ and the indwelling strength of the Holy Spirit.

GRADUAL—A hymn sung or said after the reading of the Epistle.

HERESY—A belief which is contrary to the established faith of the Church.

HOST—The consecrated bread (wafer) used in the Holy Communion.

INCARNATION—The divine act of God who came to earth as a man in the Person of His Son, Jesus Christ.

INFALLIBILITY—The doctrine that an individual, institution, or system is free from error.

INTERCOMMUNION—A mutual acceptance of the communicants of one Church at the Holy Communion of the other.

INTINCTION—The dipping of the bread into the wine in the Holy Communion; the administration and reception of both elements at the same time.

JUDGMENT—A word which refers to our daily failures before the true righteousness of God and to the final judgment of man.

JUSTIFICATION—The restoration of a sinner to fellowship with God by repentance and firm belief in Jesus Christ, who makes the penitent acceptable in new righteousness.

KINGDOM OF GOD—A New Testament description for the rule of God in the world.

LAVABO—A ceremonial "washing" of the hands of the celebrant in the Holy Communion. A small bowl and linen towel are used for this purpose.

LECTERN—A stand for the Bible from which the lessons are read in church worship.

LECTIONARY—A list of selections from Holy Scripture appointed by the Church as lessons for daily reading.

LITANY—A general prayer or supplication said responsively by minister and people.

LITURGY—The public worship of the Church, often used to refer specifically to the Holy Communion, and generally to the fixed rules, forms, and ceremonials of Christian worship.

LOCUM TENENS—A minister who fills the place of a rector or vicar who is temporarily absent from his parish.

MANIPLE—A colored band worn on the left arm with the Eucharistic vestments.

MEDIATOR—One who by his friendly offices restores cordial relations between two hostile or estranged persons.

MINISTER IN CHARGE—The title sometimes given to a locum tenens or another minister placed in charge of a parish or mission.

MITRE—A headpiece worn by a bishop.

OBLATION—An offering, specifically the sacramental offerings in the Holy Communion.

OCTAVE—A festival plus the seven days which follow.

OFFICE—A prescribed form of service used in worship, e.g., Morning Prayer.

ORDINAL—The section of the Book of Common Prayer which contains "The Form and Manner of Making, Ordaining, and Consecrating Bishops, Priests, and Deacons, according to the Order of the Protestant Episcopal Church in the United States of America."

PALL—(1) The cover which is spread over a casket during a funeral service in the church. (2) A covering for the chalice in the Holy Communion.

PARISHIONER—A member of a parish or mission.

PATEN—The plate used for the bread in the Holy Communion.

PENITENCE—A feeling or state of concern and sorrow for sin or offenses.

POST-COMMUNION—The part of the service of the Holy Communion following the communion of the people (see Book of Common Prayer, pp. 83-84).

POSTULANT—One who has been accepted by a bishop as a candidate for the ministry.

PRESIDING BISHOP—A bishop in the Protestant Episcopal Church who is elected to preside over the General Convention, the House of Bishops, and the National Council.

PRIEST—A fully ordained minister in the Church of God (see Book of Common Prayer, p. 546). The word is a shortening of the Greek word *presbyteros,* meaning "elder."

PROPITIATION—The satisfaction for, or the "covering" of, sin by God's pardon, assuring man's reconciliation to God through Jesus Christ our Mediator.

PROTESTANT—A word used to describe Christian groups who "protested" against Roman Catholicism, and generally all churches immediately or remotely related to the Reformation.

PURIFICATOR—A small linen napkin used to wipe Communion vessels.

RECONCILIATION—The restoration of the harmonious relationship between God and man accomplished by God in Jesus Christ.

RECTOR—A priest who is in charge of a parish church.

REDEMPTION—The divine work of Jesus Christ who through His death upon the Cross delivered man from sin and its consequences.

REPENTANCE—A complete turning of a penitent from sin with a resolve not to sin in the same manner again.

RESURRECTION—The divine act by which God raised Christ from the dead with the promise that Christians too shall be raised.

REVELATION—The manner or form in which God makes His reality, nature, and presence known to man.

REVEREND, THE—The title given to an ordained minister. "Reverend" is an adjective and should be used only with the article and the full name (the Reverend John Smith). See note on page 215, "How to Address a Clergyman."

REVEREND, THE RIGHT—The title given to a bishop.

REVEREND, THE MOST—The title given to an archbishop or the Presiding Bishop.

REVEREND, THE VERY—The title given to a dean.

ROCHET—A long white linen vestment worn by a bishop.

ROGATION DAYS—The three days before Ascension Day, observed as days of preparation for the festival. Special prayers ask God for fruitful fields.

SACRISTY—The room where the "sacred things," i.e., vestments and Communion vessels, of the parish church are kept and prepared for use.

SALVATION—The divine deliverance of man from sin and death through the Atonement of Jesus Christ.

SIN—Any attitude or action by which man rebels against or denies God. The General Confession admits sin "by thought, word, and deed" (see Book of Common Prayer, p. 75).

STOLE—A long narrow colored band worn over the surplice from the shoulders.

SURPLICE—A white outer vestment worn by clergy over the cassock.

TEMPTATION—A solicitation to sin by inner self-impulse or outward attraction.

THEOLOGY—A study of the beliefs concerning God and of related doctrines.

TIPPET—A long black scarf worn by clergy in the choir Offices.

TRESPASS—A legal term referring to a violation of the personal rights and property of others. In the Lord's Prayer the word *trespasses* means violations of God's law.

UNCTION—The act of ministering to the sick by anointing with oil or by the laying on of hands (see Book of Common Prayer, p. 320).

VEIL—A covering for the Communion vessels.

VENERABLE, THE—The title given to an archdeacon ("worthy of veneration").

VERGER—(1) One who carries the rod or staff before a bishop or other dignitary in procession. (2) The person in charge of taking care of the interior of a church building.

VICAR—A minister who has charge of a diocesan or parochial mission representing the bishop or the rector.

WAFER—The unleavened bread used in the Holy Communion.

How to Address a Clergyman

The three titles commonly used are:
  Father—A title affectionately used for a priest as the "father" of the whole parish family.
  Mister—A title commonly and universally used for a gentleman.
  Doctor—A title used only when the priest has received a doctor's degree.
In direct address, either "Father Smith," "Mister Smith," or "Doctor Smith" (whichever applies) should be used. These terms may also be used when speaking informally about a clergyman; formal reference is made to "the Reverend Father (*or* Mister, *or* Doctor) Smith." Letters are addressed to "The Reverend John J. Smith," and the salutation reads "Dear Fr. (*or* Mr., *or* Dr.) Smith."

Index

For definitions of some words, see "A Short Glossary of Key Words for Episcopalians," pages 205-215. Words in the Glossary are not included in this Index unless they also appear in the text of the book.